FUNNY BUSINESS

An Outsider's Year in Japan

FUNNY BUSINESS

An Outsider's Year in Japan

GARY J. KATZENSTEIN

The events and places in this story are real, as are the individuals.
However, many names have been changed or last names omitted.

Library of Congress Cataloging-in-Publication Data

Katzenstein, Gary J., 1956-
Funny business: an outsider's year in Japan/
Gary J. Katzenstein.—1st ed.
p.   cm.
Bibliography: p.
ISBN 1-56947-203-3
1. Sonī Kabushiki Kaisha—Employees.
2. Japan—Social life and customs—1945—
3. Corporate culture—Japan.   4. Katzenstein, Gary, 1956-.
I. Title.
HD9696.A3J3623   1989
338.7'6213'092dc20
[B]   89-11548   CIP

Manufactured in the United States of America

First Edition

Design and composition by The Sarabande Press

To Mom and Dad

CONTENTS

FUNNY BUSINESS

An Outsider's Year in Japan

ONE

ON THE LUCE

It was my first morning in Japan. I awoke in a closet-size room with a plastic bathroom compartment and hurriedly dressed. Mr. Morton, the head of the Asia Foundation's Tokyo office, was picking me up to escort me to Sony, where I was to live and work for a year. I extricated myself from my tiny overnight quarters and rushed downstairs. He arrived promptly.

Mr. Morton was an elderly gentleman in his mid-seventies, broad shouldered and portly, yet distinguished. He carried himself stiffly erect and walked with measured steps, observing the world from an almost expressionless face, his hawklike eyes taking in everything. He looked formidable and had little to say. What he did utter was proffered slowly, in a cadence unlike American or even British speech. The man's taciturn demeanor and formality bore witness to the half century he had lived in Japan. What little conversation I was able to manage was awkward and forced; he made me feel uneasy.

The taxi door opened automatically at the driver's touch of a button as the man bounded out of his seat to help with the luggage, of which I had a good deal. After all, a year's worth of personal effects for a six-foot-tall American was no small matter. My suitcases were crammed into the trunk and my backpack wedged onto my lap. Mr. Morton rested his glance upon me for a moment and ordered us into motion.

Despite our punctual start, Tokyo's rush-hour traffic impeded our progress. We were crawling. I gazed silently out the window; Mr. Morton looked straight ahead. Most of the neighborhoods we passed through were jammed with two- and three-story homes and shops, and masses of workers hurrying to their appointed places. Space was at such a premium that the narrow back streets had no formal sidewalks. Instead, white lines painted on the tarmac cordoned off pedestrian lanes, although cars crossed these often enough to make walking hazardous. Everything looked so exotic.

●

It had taken months of essays and interviews and anxious preparation, but I was finally on the threshold of my great adventure: a year's intimate exposure to Japanese corporate culture as a Luce Scholar, a year spent inside one of the world's best-known companies.

I was going to study Japanese management at Sony, the international electronics giant. Everyone in Japan knew the legend of Akio Morita: How he founded a small firm on the seventh floor of a burnt out department store, taking *sonus,* the Latin word for "sound," and combining it with a favorite expression, "Sonny Boy"—Sony!—to create the company name. How he licensed some neglected American technology, and how, unable to interest U.S. companies in his product ideas, he manufactured the first transistorized radios himself.

Morita parlayed that startup into an international giant. Practically everyone knew the story, like Washington's chopping down the cherry tree. It portrayed him, along with men like Toyoda-san, as one of the founding fathers of Japan's postwar rebirth.

From the transistor radio to the Trinitron color television, Sony had earned a reputation for innovation and leadership in a nation whose business practices had created tremendous success and profits. To work in such a firm for a year, for me, with a brand-new M.B.A. and M.S. in computer science from UCLA, was a dream come true. With all that I had learned about the theories and splendors of Japanese management, I was dying to see the real thing for myself.

From several thousand applicants, The Henry Luce Foundation (named for the *Time* Magazine founder) had culled fifteen of us to work for a year in the Far East, our adventure to be facilitated by another organization, the Asia Foundation. Although our interests and training varied, we all shared one unusual qualification required by the Luce Foundation: None of us had formally studied Asia or had any firsthand knowledge of the region. We knew almost nothing about the Far East. We had no preconceptions, no biases, which seemed to be the idea. Despite an eight-week cram course in Japanese and much reading in the business arts of Japan, I knew very little. Like the others who had applied, I coupled great curiosity about Japan with boundless ignorance. My personal knowledge of the country was limited to what I had casually learned from a Japanese roommate in business school and from a young lady whom I had dated, although both were much more interested in things American than in satisfying my curiosity about Japan.

Of the fifteen chosen to go to Asia, there were eleven men and four women: an architect, two journalists, three medical students, a fledgling political scientist, a few businesspeople, and a public-health specialist. All of us were highly educated, over-confident, and American. Four of us were to live in Japan: Joel, a young doctor assigned to a Japanese geriatric hospital; Ann, posted to an architectural firm; Ken, interning in the office of a parliament member; and me, Mr. Sony.

We had hoped for some practical on-site advice from the Asia Foundation to help us in our everyday lives. So far all we had been told was that we were not to pose as fashion models, if approached, and not to be surprised if we were, because Western features were considered modern-looking and therefore admired.

The reality of it was barely catching up to me. We had just spent two weeks in Hong Kong being oriented. The Crown Colony in summer had been quite an experience in itself, and was a marked contrast to our first taste of Japan. In Hong Kong, my elegantly appointed hotel room faced a combination sweat-shop and dormitory. In one of its steamy rooms Chinese work-ers slaved over sewing machines, in the adjoining room others slept on cots. Every open window revealed clutter and crowd-ing: people cooking dinner and watching television in the glare of a single inadequate light bulb. I sat in the comfortable opu-lence of my hotel, in the hyperchilled air, watching the noise and density on the other side of the glass. Not even the room's heavy air-conditioning could keep out the unique smell that permeated everything.

At the Hong Kong airport we said our good-byes: one of our group cried; another, heading for a dictatorship, gave away any books that might be construed as provocative; all sagged under the burden of the merciless heat. The four of us bound for Tokyo looked forward to the serene splendor of Mt. Fuji and the state-of-the-art society of Nippon. We weren't disappointed.

From the second we entered the terminal at Narita Airport in Tokyo, the contrast was self-evident. The aerodrome was like Japan: coolly efficient, sleek, ingeniously designed down to the last detail. The doors opened automatically as we approached.

There were at least six means of transport from the airport to downtown. The most expensive, a taxi, would run over a hundred dollars, we had been warned. Young and tightly budgeted, we opted for the bus. We purchased tickets for the 7:02 P.M. trip and put our baggage in the designated spot. The bus arrived; white-gloved porters loaded the luggage as we boarded; the bus pulled away. It was 7:02 P.M.

The public-address system aboard gave forth recorded messages in English telling us everything we could possibly want to know about the trip to town, the airport itself, and the city. As the announcements subsided, I sank into my lush seat and listened to my Walkman. In the distance Tokyo's Disneyland glided past.

With a New Yorker's survival instinct, I prepared to battle for a cab upon reaching the bus terminal. But there was no jostling, no rancor, only orderly lines. Two taxis picked up the four of us and off we went. The sweet, clean air of Tokyo felt crisp, almost autumnal. The city's twinkling lights, the measured expanse of land around the Emperor's Palace, the elegance of the illuminated Tokyo Tower, restored in me a sense of order that had been overwhelmed by the chaos of Hong Kong. The population density was obviously just as great but here there was order. I was overcome with relief and a profound sense of security. Japan was a place where things worked.

●

M r. Morton cleared his throat to announce our arrival at the gate to Sony's headquarters. Our taxi stopped before a vast building. Mr. Morton spoke briefly with the white-gloved guard, then indicated we should get out, which we did. Since he had arranged my position at Sony, I expected that he would accompany me farther. He did not. Instead, he shook my hand, wished me the best — "Call if there are any problems." — and promptly got back in the cab. There was something intimidating about Mr. Morton and I wondered if perhaps he was a holdover from the days when (as we had been casually told back in Princeton during our preparatory course) the Asia Foundation had been totally subsidized by the C.I.A. The driver-activated door closed by itself, the car pulled away.

"Hello, I am Mr. Saito," a voice announced.

Mr. Saito was a young man in blue pants, white shirt, and a peculiar gray vest.

"I will be your main contact in the Personnel Department," he said in heavily accented English.

Surrounded by my bags, I gaped at the endless cinder-block austerity of industrial Tokyo and watched the taxi, carrying Mr. Morton, fade from view.

●

M y indoctrination began like that of any newcomer to the firm. I was escorted into an enormously long, open room, filled with desks and workers, and I was offered a seat next to one of them.

Saito-san sat down at the desk and said, "Congratulations, you are now a Sony trainee." He beamed. I smiled back. A senior manager appeared alongside us and we rose for introductions. He was the director of the entire Personnel Department.

After a cursory greeting, he retired to his tiny office, one of a handful on the entire floor.

For any new Japanese employee, the first impression, the first day, is a watershed. You walk in a blank slate to be written on by the firm, indoctrinated and socialized in the ways of the company. New, fresh, with no previous business allegiances (and no possible comparisons), you are expected to give yourself over to the group, to be molded to think "the Sony way." In return, the company bestows security, benefits, and even identity.

From that first moment the line is drawn between yourself, within the company, and all those outside it. Sony employees and facilities were within; anything or anyone outside its embrace was simply outside and to be dealt with differently.

Saito-san recounted a brief history of the company, explained its configuration, described its product lines, and handed me a book, *The Sony Story*. Rules and regulations followed, forms and checkpoints along the route of my processing into the firm. I was issued a Sony uniform—a gray vest with detachable sleeves. It had been created by Issey Miyake, one of the country's foremost fashion designers.

"Everyone," Saito-san said, "from the mail boy to the chairman of the board himself, wears his uniform while on the premises." (Why had I brought all those jackets and suits?)

The vest was comfortable, if a little strange, but the color was rather drab. That might have been the intention; no one stands out wearing gray.

"Work starts promptly at eight-thirty. The gates close then. If you are late, your supervisor will have to be notified and called down to let you in. Lunch is forty-five minutes. There is a ten-minute rest period at three. The day ends at five-thirty."

Saito-san produced a rotary wheel with ten cards on it, sort of like a Rolodex. They were my location cards, he explained, and were to be set to indicate my whereabouts whenever I left my desk. I flipped through them. In rudimentary Japanese were the words for bathroom, meeting, and so on. If I was away from my desk for more than thirty minutes without properly setting my location card, my name would be announced over the public-address system and the infraction noted in my records.

"Even Akio Morita, the inventor of the Walkman, who is chairman of the board, was himself cited for a card infraction."

I had the momentary feeling that I was joining a paramilitary organization; "trainee" was beginning to sound like a euphemism for buck private.

After three long hours of this preliminary indoctrination, I was shown the latest and greatest Sony products; after that Saito-san escorted me to the company dormitory where I would reside for the duration.

Most large companies in Japan have dormitories for their unmarried male employees, and some provide housing for couples and even families. Dorms also house employees temporarily transferred from other branches and sometimes accommodate corporate guests. Sony had more than thirty such residences in the Tokyo area. Mine was a five-minute walk from headquarters, where I expected to work.

When the accommodations had been first offered, I hadn't been eager to accept. But it would have been difficult for me to find an apartment in a country where I didn't read the language or speak it fluently, so knowing in advance that I would have a place to live was reassuring. Rejection of the offer might also be insulting, I feared, so I had politely accepted their hospitality.

The rent, $125 a month, was very reasonable; for full-fledged employees it was even cheaper. After hearing about the horrors of Tokyo's housing situation, I was sure I had made the right decision. Remembering my college days, I told myself it would be a great way to make friends and have an authentically Japanese experience.

Takanawadai Dorm was a drab, three-story building in a fairly well-to-do neighborhood of southern Tokyo. Nothing marked it as a dormitory except a small sign at the entrance gate set in a seven-foot-high surrounding wall of stucco. A narrow walk led to the entrance; rust streaked the stucco walls. I didn't want to think it, but its aspect was prisonlike.

Inside the front door stretched a cold slab of hard flooring and a long dark hallway. The obligatory cubbyholes for shoes were mostly empty. Saito-san and I were discarding our footwear when out popped a middle-aged couple, bowing and smiling and uttering an effusion of greetings. Saito-san introduced me to Mr. and Mrs. Hashimoto, the dorm keepers. They spoke no English. If I needed anything, I would have to ask for it in Japanese.

The dorm housed about eighty employees, all unmarried of course, and all, including myself, in their twenties. The room assigned was one for company guests or short-time residents, 102B. Bags dangling from my limbs, I trudged down the hall to my new home.

A shared foyer area held two closets. In my actual room there was no furniture except for a low writing desk, a Sony Trinitron television, and the customary tatami mats on the floor. It was a four-tatami-mat room, measuring six feet by twelve feet—not a luxurious accommodation even by Japanese standards. There was no space for a bed. Instead, I had a futon, not what passed in the States for one, but the real kind—a pair of padded quilts, one for warmth, one to lie on. The futon was to be laid out each night and stored away in the large closet during the day.

The hard floor would be good for my back, I decided, and the quilts warm. Besides, rolling up a futon would be far easier than making a bed every day. It made sense: In a room exactly as wide as I was tall, space would be at a premium.

The pillow was another matter. The traditional Japanese pillow, made of bamboo, had an hourglass shape. The head and neck rested on hard bamboo in the curve. Somehow I didn't care how therapeutic it might be, it just looked hideously uncomfortable.

To make absolutely certain that I could find my way to work the next morning, Saito-san walked me back to headquarters along the city streets. There he quickly said good-bye, explaining that he had overtime to do.

After making my way back to the dormitory, I wandered through the halls. Poking my head into the occasional open doorway, I had some one-sided chats in my primitive Japanese. In almost every room cartons of books were stacked atop files, atop storage boxes, atop whatever else didn't fit in the foyer closets. Ties and jackets hung from hooks on the walls, and from clotheslines strung wall to wall dangled shirts and pants on hangers. The residents I spoke to were friendly, but their English and my Japanese were not good enough for anything beyond the most simple exchanges. When I realized that only two or three men in the entire dorm spoke conversational English, I suddenly sensed how "Japanese" my dormitory existence would be.

Returning to my room, I set about unpacking. My two large suitcases were filled with clothes for all climatic conditions. And I had packed both suits and sports jackets, not sure which would be appropriate for wear at the office. Now, with my all-purpose gray vest, I realized I needn't have bothered.

I had a substantial amount of clothing and it had to go somewhere. A huge closet inside the room looked promising but was for storing my futon during the day. The narrow closet in the foyer, on the other hand, was more like a locker, with a bar for hangers. But there were no chests, dresser drawers, or shelves.

In my handy pocket dictionary I found the word for "shelf."

"Where are the shelves for this closet?" I asked Hashimoto-san, the dorm keeper. He rustled up one. It helped, but there was no way my wardrobe would fit in the space available.

A door opened across the tiny hall and an eye peered out, warily. My foyer-mate had been aroused by our activity. I was introduced. He was in his late twenties, on temporary assignment from Sony-Osaka, and spoke only a few words of English, I was sorry to learn. As everyone watched, I hung up whatever coats, suits, and jackets I could in my foyer closet; put some items on the single shelf; and made leaning piles of my pants, shirts, socks, and underwear, stacking them in the space not covered by the futon. When I saw that my neighbor's foyer closet was nearly empty, I asked if I could use some of his space, too. He readily agreed and I happily began transferring the overflow from my modest room. However, when Mr. and Mrs. Hashimoto saw what was happening, they became agitated. My closet, they informed me, was on the left; my foyer-mate's, on the right. I politely explained that my neighbor had agreed to the arrangement.

Hashimoto-san stood firm. "Rules are rules. They are not to be broken." Under his stern gaze I piled the offending items back onto the floor of my room.

TWO

OH, SONY BOY

Before starting for work my first day, I took advantage of the subsidized Sony cafeteria. Workers at Sony could buy nutritious and tasty meals for about half what they would cost on the outside.

I figured I'd better stick with something I knew: toast, eggs, and milk. Even so, the milk was thick and gloppy, like superrich English "double cream," and I could barely swallow it. When I cracked my hard-boiled egg it went splat and wound up all over my pants. The egg was raw.

Several people around me laughed, covering their mouths, but most had their eyes glued to "O Shin," an immensely popular TV soap opera, and were oblivious to my embarrassment. A man came over with some towels. He explained that raw eggs are part of a traditional Japanese breakfast, the topping on a bowl of rice, seaweed, and soy sauce.

After a quick trip back to the dorm to change, I hurried once again to the Sony complex. There were sites all around the city and its outskirts. This, the headquarters compound, consisted of perhaps a dozen buildings, some connected by overhead walkways. They looked like rehabilitated factory buildings or warehouses, except for the brand-new Research Division.

Still, I fantasized the opulent interiors that I was certain were behind the typically pallid Japanese exteriors. I thought of the sleek, functional designs of their many products and was actually looking forward to the antiseptic serenity of a modern office in the company's Computer Division.

Saito-san escorted me. I was introduced to Yoshino-san, my immediate supervisor, and shown the offices of the division. There were 130 people split into teams and all housed in two huge rooms, eighty in one, fifty in the other. Yoshino-san was in charge of a twelve-person team and introduced me to them: six men and six women. I was lucky thirteen.

The massive room I would be working in was ugly. It was perhaps half the length of a football field, twenty yards wide, and windowless. The building had indeed been a factory, with overhead pipes and utility cables left exposed. Poor air circulation and the lack of windows made the office a steam bath. As large as the floor space was, every inch was crammed full. Computer terminals and their accessories lined the walls. Desks were piled high with a random clutter of books and papers; some had barely enough uncovered space on them to accommodate even a single sheet of paper. The lack of carpeting or barriers between the eight clusters of desks made the noise level so high that telephone calls would be a real challenge to make, and concentration on work nearly impossible. Not even the managers had their own offices; they simply sat at one end of the grouped desks occupied by their subordinates. Privacy was not a consideration. In a small concession to the need for quiet, a "coding room" had been set aside for writing computer programs. This was segregated into six cubicles with six seats. Although occupants were plainly visible, a magnetic nameplate, issued each employee, was required to be posted to identify a cubicle's occupant.

I said something to my new boss, but he did not respond. Saito-san explained that Yoshino-san didn't speak English. I nodded at him instead, a nervous Westerner's variation on a Japanese bow. No English, I thought. Right.

Mr. Takagi came forward. Takagi-san would be my interpreter and my liaison. Of my dozen immediate co-workers, only he and the assistant manager, Kamakura-san, spoke any English. Takagi-san's desk adjoined mine. He offered his hand for a limp handshake and said, in an unenthusiastic monotone, "Our team is very lucky because you are the first and only foreigner in the Computer Division."

I was taken to meet Murata-bucho, the division's general manager.

"Hello, and welcome to Sony," he said in nearly perfect English. "You are very lucky to work for such a fine company as Sony. Neither the Research Division nor any other Sony division wanted you. But I was willing to give you a chance."

It sounded rather as if he were bestowing charity. And his pronouncement struck a chord. I had initially been informed that I would be working in Sony's Research Division. Just before I left Hong Kong I had received a two-line telegram informing me that there had been a change. Despite my disappointment, I assumed that someone had decided my particular skills would make this placement more valuable to the firm. Perhaps they had a special project for me to work on. Now I left the division head's office thinking I had been wrong to make such an assumption.

When I returned to my group, Takagi-san had a detailed schedule of my assignments for me. He said, "As you are a trainee—"

"I suppose I am, at Sony," I interrupted, "but I do have two master's degrees and considerable computer experience."

"I see," he said, paused, and, referring to my schedule, began again. "As you are a trainee at Sony, first you will get an overview of the company, then learn Sony COBOL, then study the manufacturing system . . ." Takagi-san droned on. I was flabbergasted.

The chart of my coming months covered every conceivable moment, right up to my departure, months hence. Also, the projects assigned to me were curious. Whoever compiled them must have closely followed my résumé, which listed experience and jobs going back ten years, and, on the basis of it, had assumed interests that coincided with the skills demanded by those jobs. My résumé, however, was simply a record of work performed and college jobs held, not a blueprint of what I had hoped to see and do in Japan, or in my professional life. Still, I had come to Tokyo to observe and to learn, not to tell them how to run their business. The last thing I wanted was to get off on the wrong foot, so I decided to go with the flow.

I sat at my desk to review the work chart. Takagi-san handed me some papers as well. I looked them over, but it was hopeless. They were all in Japanese.

•

Takagi-san invited me to lunch with three other male colleagues and I accepted. In the commissary, he gave me instructions about how to buy my food and then how to find him among the diners. Our allotted time was forty-five minutes. I paid for my food and inched past the cashier. Before me was a sea of Asians, all in gray uniforms, all with the same black hair, sitting at countless long tables eating bowls of rice with beef and slurping noodles. Takagi-san was somewhere out there. I laughed at the futility of trying to locate him. Fortunately, he saw me wandering around, my head sticking up a foot above everyone else's, and he came to claim me, like a parent fetching a bewildered lost child in a crowded department store.

Lunchtime I figured would be for socializing and relaxing, but my host and his friends ate in silence, hurrying their meal so as to get back to work. We ate and rushed back to our desks.

At precisely three o'clock music came over the public-address system and everyone rose to do the daily exercises. I, too, stood alongside my desk and self-consciously went through the stretches, hopping, jumping jacks, and neck gyrations that constituted the usual routine. Although I did not understand much of the instruction, I mimicked my co-workers and, after a while, caught on.

After exercises we had green tea and snacks in our work area. The women, I saw, were in charge of making tea, buying and serving refreshments, and cleaning up afterward. The men sat back and relaxed.

A *kaigi,* or meeting, of my group was held in a conference area set off from the rest of the floor by thin walls. The purpose of the meeting was for us all to get acquainted. This was a set procedure for getting to know someone in a business setting and so it was quite formal, as though I were interviewing for a job.

Takagi-san opened the get-to-know-me meeting with the suggestion that I describe my education, and I did so.

"How old are you?" someone asked.

"Twenty-seven."

"Will you," a young woman asked, "continue your schooling upon your return?"

Her name was Maruyama-san. She was just over five feet, slender, with glossy hair worn short. I smiled and attempted to tell her in Japanese that if I resumed studies when I returned home, I would become a *hakasei,* a Ph.D. Unfortunately, I said *hakuchi* by mistake and got some strange looks—*hakuchi* is the word for "idiot."

They asked me my name, my height, weight, eye color, and my date of birth. I answered every question.

Imai-san asked, "Have you left your wife and your children behind in the United States?"

I explained that I wasn't married.

Maruyama-san raised her pinky. "Do you have a girlfriend?"

There was an outburst of feminine giggling, barely suppressed by hands placed over mouths. I said I was an unattached bachelor.

They looked astonished. "Really?" they chorused.

Someone asked me my blood type, one of the few questions that didn't startle me. This I had been prepared for. In Japan, blood type was equivalent to one's astrological sign in the United States. Someone else asked for my hand and studied my palm, reading the lines there—to know me better, they said. Several of the women peered at my hand and traced various creases. I had been born, they informed me, in the year of the monkey.

With these important items taken care of, the final bit of business was to give me a suitable Japanese name. Katzenstein is hard enough to say in English. In Japan, where some sounds in my name did not exist, pronouncing it was an absolute disaster. The solution was to call me Gary-san. Gay-ree-sahn they pronounced it. My welcoming party, I was informed as the meeting broke up, would be held later that week.

I asked Maruyama-san why she had raised her pinky when

she'd posed her question about my marital status. A raised pinky, she explained, designated a girlfriend; a raised thumb, a boyfriend.

"I like to learn about foreign countries," she said, "particularly America. Please don't hesitate to ask me if you have any questions or problems."

•

The bathing room at the dormitory was traditional Japanese, with wooden floors, benches, a good-size changing room, clothes cubby, toilets and urinals, sinks, and, beyond a sliding door, a huge communal tub the size of a small and shallow swimming pool. The tub was filled only once at the beginning of the evening, so it was imperative not to enter until you had cleaned yourself.

Proper etiquette required that one wash first while sitting on a little stool or inverted bucket in front of a row of faucets that surrounded the tub. Here one brushed one's teeth and spat out, onto the floor. The faucets were only two feet off the ground and could hardly be used as showers. Each had a mirror for shaving while seated. You would lather yourself up, then, to rinse off, you had to pour buckets of water over your head. Two spigots had rubber hoses and shower heads attached, but only one hose was long enough to use as a makeshift, standup shower. The trick with the buckets of water was to properly mix the hot and the cold and avoid temperatures of either extreme that might invite cardiac arrest. Once clean, you were entitled to submerge yourself in the nearly boiling water, with everyone else.

There was a real art to this. The tub was some thirty inches deep. All the Japanese slid easily into it with satisfied looks on their faces, welcoming the familiar warmth. For those unused to the scalding temperature of the water, the first few seconds were agony. The trick was not to react to the pain and thrash around, because that just circulated and replenished the boiling liquid. The thing to do was not move. After a few moments your body would actually cool off the water immediately surrounding you, rendering it tolerable. I sat there like a tea bag, gritting my teeth, watching the men around me bask in the scalding water.

This ritual, indulged in four nights a week, was a silent activity undertaken with a purposefulness that belied its ostensible goal of relaxation. In a sense it was a purification ceremony intended to cleanse oneself of the day's physical and mental demands before replenishing mind and body with a night's rest.

I didn't exactly enjoy the bucket shower or the scalding bath, but it helped me to see that there was a very definite personal schedule in the dormitory that I needed to conform to. It had some idiosyncracies. I found out, the hard way, that there was no hot water whatsoever on Saturdays. Could I, however, learn the rules and ropes with no one to explain them to me?

By observing, I had picked up quite a lot. For instance, the basins had only cold-water taps. One did not wash one's face at the sink. Hands were washed in the sink, albeit in cold water, which did not seem particularly hygienic to me. Nor did brushing one's teeth and spitting out on the floor in the area around the huge tub, but that was the accepted procedure.

There were no electric outlets for shavers for the simple reason that Japanese men don't need to shave daily. When my dormmates did shave, they did so while sitting on the buckets used at bath time and disposing of the lather and whiskers on the floor.

The most urgent problem of personal hygiene confronting me was laundry. I had neglected the matter in Hong Kong and was now down to my last pair of underpants. Snooping around the dorm's darker corners, I looked for washing machines but found only a tiny thing, a primitive 1950s-style model that could handle maybe three shirts and a couple of pairs of socks at one time. The teensy washer may have been the perfect match for the typical Japanese wardrobe, but with my huge backlog, it wasn't going to help much.

I consulted the dorm keeper, Hashimoto-san, about an alternative to the dinky machine. He directed me to a laundromat some distance from the dormitory. Or else I could use the dorm's dry-cleaning service.

That would be fine for outer wear, of course, and for removing the egg stain from my trousers, but my immediate concern, I explained, was underwear. Hashimoto-san shrugged. The dry-cleaning service was quick and efficient, he insisted. My garments would be back the next day. I surrendered and he summoned the dry cleaner to pick up my underwear. It reappeared the next day, dry-cleaned and precisely pressed.

Toilets required another minor social adjustment. Instead of the sit-down Western variety, Japanese lavatories had elongated ceramic holes in the floor over which one squatted. A little hood at one end indicated the front, I learned.

While squatting did not present an insurmountable problem, there was the question of what to do with your lowered trousers. Close observation of others seemed ill advised so I struggled along, not quite sure whether pants should be completely removed or whether just being careful was customary. It was a question I could not get up the nerve to ask anyone.

●

The evening of my welcoming dinner, my workmates and I all left the office together, piled into taxis, and headed for a restaurant in the Akasaka Mitsuke district.

Norita-san sat on one side of me in the cab, Takagi-san on the other. As usual, I wanted to know everything about everything. Norita-san said, "Gary-san, if you want to get to understand us, you have to remember that we Japanese are all the same."

I tried to challenge this. Surely he couldn't mean it literally. But Takagi-san was quick to agree, adding, "You must remember, ours is an island country."

I nodded without really knowing what he meant by this. What I had noticed, however, was that they were using a different *we* from the formal one I had been taught. This *we* made a distinction between all Japanese and those not Japanese.

We drove through what seemed like a typhoon, accosted by rain and thunder and tremendous slashes of lightning. Arriving at the restaurant, we dashed from the taxi to the entrance. There the way seemed barred by a man making shooing gestures at me, as if to chase me off. But Takagi-san stepped in front of me, assuring me that our host was in fact greeting us, that his dismissive gesture was actually one of welcome.

We left umbrellas and shoes by the door. As I changed to slippers and looked down at the long line of identical black lace-ups, I was glad to be a foreigner with big feet. At least my foot gear stood out and I would be sure of wearing my own home that night.

The restaurant was gorgeous, decorated like an elegant Japanese mansion of the nineteenth century, with rooms divided by shoji screens that could be opened to create a larger space or closed for privacy. When we reached the rear room set aside for our party, we removed our slippers before stepping onto the tatami mats encircling the low table.

"Konbanwa, minna-san," I said, remembering a simple polite phrase.

The response from my fellow celebrants was immediate: "Anato no nihongo ga jozu desune." Which meant: "Your Japanese is very good." But it wasn't, and I knew it by now. They were just being Japanese, saying the right thing, being well mannered.

The long tables before us were laden with platters of sushi and sashimi interspersed with bottles of beer. I helped myself to some tuna sushi and saw that all eyes were on me. Some of the women squealed in astonishment.

"Can you really eat sushi?" Kaneko-san asked, quite seriously.

"Of course," I said. "I like it."

She looked amazed. "And you use chopsticks?"

I demonstrated my prowess with them to her delight. She covered her mouth and giggled.

"We weren't sure foreigners could really eat sushi or use chopsticks," she said.

When I began pouring myself a beer, Fujita-san snatched the bottle away.

"No, no. I will pour," he insisted. "In Japan, people always pour beer for each other. It is a way of showing our regard for one another."

He filled my glass. Since custom also required a glass to remain full to the brim, this was a service he had to perform several times as the dinner progressed. After a bit, I rose to look for the bathroom. It was only a few steps from our enclosure and I started toward it.

"Your slippers! Put on your slippers!" they all screamed in horror. "You must not walk on the floor without your slippers." I jumped back onto the tatami mats and quickly donned my slippers, then set out again. As I crossed the threshold into the men's room, more screams greeted me: "Take them off!" I must have looked as puzzled as I felt. "Put on rubber slippers, rubber slippers!"

I looked down. At my feet were rubber slippers. I slipped out of my cloth slippers and into a pair of these.

In the bathroom the commode was the native ceramic hole that I was struggling to master. Typical, too, was the absence of any sort of towels or air dryers. The custom was to dry your hands with your very own handkerchief and carry the wet hanky away with you. This was going to take some getting used to, I thought, tucking the wet cloth back in my pocket.

On my trip back to our table, I managed the footwear exchanges in the proper sequence, wary of provoking another outcry. While I knew, of course, that Japanese don't wear shoes in their homes and in many social settings, I hadn't realized the extent of their concern with footwear. Somehow I had violated decorum several times over in a matter of a few feet.

Some of my teammates at Sony took off their shoes each morning when they arrived at the office and switched to sandals, but I was learning the hard way that how you were shod depended upon what area you were entering and that each type of covering had to remain in its designated area.

There was not just a hierarchy of cleanliness involved. The place, the area to be entered, determined the informality or formality of behavior required, and one's footwear reflected that. When you had your shoes off you were inside your group's space—your social set at home, among your company colleagues at work or play. You could relax. When shoes were put on, you also raised your guard and were on your best behavior.

After our main course it was time for my formal introduction. One of my teammates made some welcoming remarks and then came the awaited moment, the evening's highlight: my speech. I stumbled over a few phrases in Japanese, pointing to myself several times to make my meaning clear. Each time I pointed, Takagi-san waved his hand violently in front of his chest. I continued on, haltingly. When I saw them wince at my Japanese pronunciation, I switched to English. Takagi-san translated the rest of my speech.

As soon as I sat down, he hastily whispered to me that pointing at one's chest is an aggressive gesture. Instead of ingratiating myself with my new teammates, I had been offering to fight them. In future, should I wish to refer to myself, I should do so by pointing to my nose. Chagrined, I nodded.

As the evening wound on, the men became quite drunk. The women remained properly sober. Looking around, I realized we had polished off all the liquor and I was very thirsty. Nohara-san offered to get me something to quench my thirst.

He brought back a can and, handing it to me, said, "Here, this is a unique Japanese soft drink."

"What makes it unique?" I said.

"Taste it and you'll see."

I did. The liquid was frothy and white and tasted like a mixture of lemon, lime, and grapefruit. It was strangely bitter.

"What's it called?" I asked, staring at the can.

"Cow piss."

I choked.

"Here," he said, "you can read it on the can."

I read it out phonetically: "Cal-pico."

"Don't worry," Takagi-san chortled. "It's not what you fear it might be. It's a carbonated calcium drink."

After a while we had drunk so much that everything seemed amusing. We started comparing animal noises in Japanese and

English. A Japanese dog, I learned, goes *won won*. A cat, *neow*. A cow emits a long, deep *moe*. A rooster crows *ko-key-ko-ko*.

Dinner concluded with "closing ceremonies." Kamakura-san wished me the best of luck and, on the count of three, they all clapped—once. I was officially at Sony.

THREE

WHO'S ON FIRST

After work one day I set out for the ballpark, but when I reached Korakuen Stadium the game was sold out. The *besubaru* season was almost over and I had wanted to catch a Tokyo Giants game, so I looked for scalpers.

I couldn't understand much of what they said, but for about $8 worth of yen I was delighted to get a ticket for a seat right behind first base. Passing through the gate, I consulted the ticket stub and began looking for section 58, row 10, seat 1. The ushers, however, kept herding me farther and farther down the right-field line. I kept going and going. Why? One of the ushers tried to explain to me in broken English that my ticket was for general admission to the bleachers.

I was furious at having been taken, or at least badly misunderstood, but I marched out to the bleachers only to find them completely full. It was standing room only, six deep in fans. Discouraged, I turned back, hoping food would help. Passing up the hot dog kiosks, I bought a roasted squid on a stick and impulsively strode toward the seats behind home plate. With great courtesy, the usher swung open the gate and pointed to some empty seats, and said politely, "Please enter and enjoy the *besubaru* game," and I did.

The Tokyo Giants were playing the Hiroshima Carp. The players bowed to each other; the game was about to begin. I glanced up at the electronic scoreboard that displayed in *kanji* characters (unintelligible to me) all the players names and a vast array of information, including wind direction and speed.

In point of fact, the Tokyo Giants, it had been explained to me, were actually the Yomiuri Giants, but they were often referred to as the Tokyo Giants because they played most of their home games in Tokyo. Like most teams, they also played a few games in other "home" cities across Japan. Their actual names were not taken from their geographic headquarters but rather from the companies that owned them, such as the Yomiuri newsfirm that owned the Giants, or the Hanshin railway company that owned the Hanshin Tigers, and the Yakult Beverage Company that owned the Yakult Swallows. The Seibu department store–railroad combine fielded the Seibu Lions. But what in the world, I wondered, were the Nippon Ham Fighters? Then I realized. They were the Fighters baseball club sponsored by the Nippon Ham Company.

The player introductions were just finishing and the crowd roared at each name. From the eruptions it was self-evident that each team's supporters sat on opposite sides of the stadium. The noise surged as the game began, with cheerleaders prancing atop the dugout roofs, exhorting their teams and flailing the air with pompoms and banners in the teams' colors (black and orange borrowed from their namesake in San Francisco), and beating on an ancient native drum. The noise level and the sections of "home" and "away" rooters reminded me more of American college football than baseball, as did the awesome crescendo that erupted as one of the Hiroshima Carp belted a home run that cleared the left-field wall. There was mass hysteria. Horns blared, people howled, toilet paper and confetti streamers arced through the night sky.

The celebrations were many. What with the smaller ballpark, dirt infield, a lively ball, and terrible pitchers who were no match for the hitters, there were lots of opportunities for shrill celebration. Several differences from American baseball practices were glaring, though. Everytime a foul or a home run carried the ball into the riotous stands, it was politely returned to the field. Propriety prevailed, even amidst hysteria. Also, no matter how obvious, the official scorers virtually refused to charge fielders with errors.

During what passed for the seventh-inning stretch, I chatted up an usher who explained about my ticket in section 58, row 10, seat 1. It wasn't my seat designation at all. The first digits, 58, were the year, the fifty-eighth of the current emperor's reign, which is how years were counted in Japan. The 10 indicated the month, this from the Western calendar, and 1 the day of the month. The numbers hadn't had anything to do with my seat.

So far, I had only seen the Western calendar in use in Japan, but now I realized that the ancient culture of Nippon was never far from the surface.

●

My routine became settled. In the mornings I would walk to work enjoying the sights and sounds of Tokyo arising. Hawkers plied their trade in the street, chanting their offer of goods. One sold toilet paper, another sweet potatoes. The garbage collectors wheeled past, picking up refuse to be recycled.

The buildings were closely situated but none was very tall, most being one or two stories. Laundry hung from many of the metal terraces that were common to private dwellings and apartment houses since dryers were rare. Bedding hung from the railings, too, as it was customary to air futons daily.

At the commissary I ate breakfast by myself while my co-workers watched television. Everyone was so well dressed. The women in designer-label suits, the men in their well-cut business suits, demure ties, shined shoes, many sporting expensive Seiko watches. A good number of these were chronographic wristwatches that had amazing functions. Muzak was piped in at 8:25 to remind us to head for our desks. In the dimly lit hall outside the Computer Division room, I took off my jacket, stowed it in my locker, and put on my gray company vest, complete with name tag, then proceeded to my workstation. As I entered I would greet those already at their desks, most already engrossed. Everyone bowed to one another, myself (shyly) included. At 8:30 a buzzer sounded and work commenced officially.

My co-workers were hard to engage in a personal way and yet they went to great lengths to take care of me now that I was part of the Sony family. When I had film to develop, Takagi-san had it done for me at Sony's insider discount; Maruyama-san heard me express interest in ikebana, flower arranging, and instantly placed a call to arrange lessons for me.

When I asked for information about aikido, a popular martial art, Takagi-san arranged for lessons and set up a session for later that very day, and even found a sweatsuit and sneakers for me that fit perfectly.

When I mentioned to my co-workers that it would be nice if I could get some practice speaking Japanese, they immediately assigned one of my teammates, Nohara-san, to partake in a hour of conversational Japanese after work. Then, in the course of our practice, when I asked about brands of soap and shampoo that he might recommend, Nohara-san insisted on accompanying me to a nearby store and personally picking out the items he thought would be best. There seemed to be no limits to the attentiveness. It was, however, also paternalistic to the point of condescension. I felt I was being looked after like a child. Their attentions were constricting.

Part of my orientation the first weeks included lectures that I was given by various department heads. It would have been a wonderful exposure to the workings of the corporation except for one small problem: The talks were in Japanese and I understood only the occasional word. Takagi-san admonished me for looking bored during the lectures and for not asking any questions. He pointed out that many were delivered by important people within the company who had spent rare spare moments preparing their talks and then briefing me.

It was awkward to explain that I just couldn't understand most of what was being said to me, even with his translations, which amounted to half a sentence every now and then. I said I appreciated their efforts, truly, but I had only begun to study Japanese that summer and I wasn't fluent. Takagi-san seemed startled but said nothing. (I was surprised, too, and wondered if Mr. Morton had somehow failed to make that clear when arranging my position.)

In point of fact, the lectures were boring, although I dared not express this opinion. What I had managed to pick up, even with my limited Japanese, was bone-dry data: charts, figures, minute statistics. Anytime I asked probing, analytical questions that took off from the sparse information being conveyed, the responses were hesitant and evasive. When mention was made of a test that all employees had to pass in order to be promoted, I innocently asked what this consisted of.

The lecturer said, "The test covers such basics as product lines and company structure. Employees must memorize sales results for Sony products, as well as various balance-sheet figures. They must also learn proper decorum, such as the type and color of pants to wear in a given situation, and—"

Another manager broke in, the explanation was dropped. I asked if I could see a copy of the test.

"It wouldn't interest you" was the reply, and we returned to the stimulating organization chart once again.

●

On Sunday I decided to do some shopping and then to visit a park. I got a subway ticket from a vending machine and got it punched by the attendant as I caught the train to Hiro Station. Exiting, one of the attendants invalidated my ticket and collected it. I wondered at the odd juxtaposition of automated ticket vending and manual double-punching and collecting.

When I had finished my shopping chores, I couldn't find the subway station and asked a passerby. "Hiro Station?" he said, looking quizzical. "No, not around here." I asked again, this time a woman. After long reflection, she motioned for me to follow and led me five blocks to a station. "Here," she said politely, then bowed and walked away.

Just to check, I asked a young man in English, "Is this Hiro Station."

"No," he began, "it's—" He stopped. "Oh," he said, "I see. You mean Hiroo. Yes, yes, it is!"

I could see that with the slightest deviation in pronunciation I would be in trouble. An evening in Los Angeles's Little Tokyo came back to me. I wanted to try out the Japanese I was intensely studying in anticipation of my trip. I tried ordering pickles in a restaurant but managed instead to ask for male genitals, much to the amused astonishment of the Japanese diners.

I took the train to Ueno Park, where an arts festival was under way. On the grounds were two concert halls, the Tokyo zoo, several museums, and the Toshogu Shrine, a complex wooden structure ringed by an exquisite Japanese garden. The footbridges and the arches were a bright red; the garden's shrubbery and rock outcroppings, all perfectly balanced. Outside, strollers wandered among the *jizo* statues, primitive stone figures wearing red caps, many with pinwheels next to them; inside, a tea ceremony was under way.

It was exactly as it had been described to us in our orientation: a highly stylized ritual with all the aesthetic Japanese elements present. Concentration. Texture. Acerbity. Scarcity. Contrast.

Each movement was done silently, with perfect attention. The ceramic bowls were turned in the celebrants' hands before drinking so they might feel the highly irregular texture of the asymmetrically colored pieces. Even the tea had its special texture as it frothed up after being stirred as it brewed. Sweets were served, just a few, each extremely sweet, the excessive sweetness contrasting sharply with the bland (sometimes bitter) tea.

Wandering down the hill from the temple, I came upon a shed. Inside were two men and two women dressed in long, dark-blue skirts and plain white blouses, the traditional dress of the warrior. One man and one woman stood motionless on the wooden floor, both facing in the same direction. I couldn't imagine what was happening. Then I heard a whoosh and a thud. Looking toward the sound of the impact, I saw targets. The two people were perfectly immobile, statues with bows in their hands. Slowly they put down their bows and left the platform. The other pair took their place with great ceremony. They selected arrows with painstaking care, then stood silent. After some moments, they raised their bows effortlessly. The man drew back the bowstring and held it poised for some time. The discipline and intensity were amazing.

The arrow flew. It shot forward and into the target's precise center. After perhaps a minute, his companion replicated his motions and similarly pierced the target's heart. Had there been no bows, no arrows, I might have mistaken it for a religious ceremony.

Tour guides passed wearing their recognizable outfits: light blue scarves, dark blue skirts, white blouses and gloves. On the lake in the park the romantic boat rowers were so numerous that their vessels could barely move.

The shogun's house in the park was made of richly textured wood, coarse stucco, rocks, translucent inner walls of paper and wood, smooth ceramic floor tiles. My eye savored the wood-block prints, a sand painting, the path in the garden. In a doorway, swaying in the breeze, hung a *noren* cloth, its motion flirting with the surrounding structure. Within the well of an interior courtyard was a Zen rock garden of dark boulders on raked white pebbles. It was perfectly silent except for moving air and a trickle of water. A bamboo rod slowly filled with water, dipped and sounded against a rock—a hollow *clop, clop, clop*. The water poured out gently; the bamboo swayed upright.

At the arts fair, female dancers dressed in kimonos chanted and danced in unison to the beat of a large drum; their motions were subtle and precise; their control, remarkable. No less remarkable were the bonsai trees on display, each perfect. But the flower arranging exhibit was what really struck me. The sheer beauty of the designs, so very simple yet powerful, were truly overwhelming. Despite the minimalism, through impeccable placement, it was as if feeling and movement had been created. I knew I hadn't time to learn the secrets of bonsai or Zen archery, but I thought I could maybe learn something of ikebana.

The art of flower arranging proved incredibly arduous—and awkward (also expensive at $35 a lesson). The classes were open to Sony employees only and conducted in one of the company buildings, on a floor set aside for employees' club activities. Here the aikido club met to practice this martial art, so, too, the karate club and, of course, my ikebana class.

I was the only foreigner, the only man, and nervous. Bowing politely to all the ladies, I took my place. Naturally, no one had said anything about the possibility of my feeling conspicuous. The method of instruction was direct yet confusing. The teacher arranged flowers. We watched. Then we tried to imitate her arrangement. There were no explanations of technique, no instructions, no discussion. We watched, we imitated, over and over again, placing our flowers in the *kabin,* the "flower bowl," precisely as the teacher demonstrated. Every arrangement had its catalytic center, sometimes a small red flower that, by its judicious placement, became the focus.

The results were impressive but the learning method tedious. I sensed something intrinsically Japanese in the rote lessons. It was as if we deliberately avoided logical analysis of what we were doing and learning, as if logical understanding would somehow interfere with the creative process, as if articulating and formulating would diminish the greater whole and reduce it to its humble parts. The flowers, the bowl, the spatial relationships simply were.

Although I watched the teacher's every move and tried to copy it, my arrangements were a far cry from hers. Yet rather than accept my efforts as a beginner's modest attempt, she came over to "add some finishing touches." With a few quick motions, she overhauled my amateurish design, transforming my humble work into a work of art.

"There," she said, "see what beauty you've created!"

There was something typically formal and even ritualistic about my "accomplishment." She prided herself on helping others; it was part of her obligation as a teacher to make sure I succeeded at ikebana. In Japan, it was awful when someone stood out by virtue of having failed; I would not fail at flower arranging. She proceeded to take several photographs of me with my "creation."

Each week I would take my bowl of flowers back to my dormitory room and place it among the many piles of clothes and books on the floor of my crowded, furnitureless room, then lie down next to it and contemplate its form. What were the blossoms trying to tell me about Nippon?

•

I practiced saying, "Which way to Tokyo Station?" so many times that I figured I had it down. Maybe I did, but when I posed the question to unsuspecting strangers, the answers were unintelligible to me. They never sounded quite the way they were supposed to. I listened to the long, elaborate answers, then meandered down the street to try someone else, and secretly hoped to find someone who spoke English. Or—as so often happened—someone would take me bodily where I wanted to go.

When I had landed in Japan, I had a solid book knowledge of beginner's grammar and a workable vocabulary. I could ask simple questions. I assumed I'd be in good shape, but I wasn't. I was still getting lost on streets and trains, and although I had learned to distinguish mah-jongg parlors from restaurants, my meals were often limited to the items written phonetically because that was all I could manage to read. Mostly I pointed at the amazingly realistic display models of food.

Sometimes at work I couldn't understand my colleagues at all. I had to master Japanese more quickly; I needed lessons. Mr. Morton recommended a language school and I signed up. Sony offered me a classroom.

On the first day my teacher, Tsurumi-sensei, arrived bearing a stack of materials. She bowed and I bowed. Tsurumi-sensei was middle-aged, conservatively dressed, an angel in disguise I hoped. We chatted briefly and set forth.

As there was no really good English-Japanese dictionary, she introduced me to the Japanese writing system so that I could use a Japanese dictionary instead. She explained that three different scripts were used: *hiragana, katakana,* and *kanji.* All three might occur in the same sentence, or even in a single word. I forced a smile.

Hiragana and *katakana* consisted of 48 characters . . . each. *Hiragana* was cursive; *katakana,* angular. *Katakana* was sometimes employed to emphasize a word written (usually) in *kanji* or *hiragana* (so far so good). Mostly it was used for words borrowed from foreign languages. Like *pan* from the Portuguese word for "bread," *mi sheen* for sewing machine, or *arbeito* from German, *eisu kureemu* from English. In fact, the whole writing system had been adopted from the Chinese. It was a rough fit. The languages—their grammar, vocabulary, pronunciations—were unrelated.

Kanji, the third script, she explained, was probably the hardest to learn. Each *kanji* character represented a different word or idea. It might be as simple as a single horizontal dash, like a minus sign, which is the number one; or a sort of plus sign, which is the *kanji* character for the number ten; or three vertical squiggles for "river," a rectangular character with a stroke across that meant "day." It all sounded reasonable enough. However, as Tsurumi-sensei continued, the degree of complexity became intimidatingly clear.

A simple *kanji* character might be one stroke, it might also be as many as forty. "Melancholy," for instance, was twenty-three strokes. How appropriate, I thought.

To read even the simplest newspaper story you had to know at least 1,850 *kanji* characters. To write any one character you had to know anywhere from one to forty strokes, and—just to make it easy—you had to "write" them in a prescribed sequence.

My head reeled with calculations of the possible total of sets any one person would have to know to master the written language. Was she talking about learning fifty thousand characters?

"*Kanji,*" she said, "are not a random collection of strokes. Each character is made in a definite order. Because we Japanese all write a character in precisely the same way, we can accurately count the number of strokes needed to make each *kanji* character."

I was awed. "How can I possibly use a *kanji* dictionary?"

"*Kanji* dictionaries are organized by certain subcharacters called radicals. These appear in many characters. In addition, they are categorized by the number of strokes comprising the character."

"Right," I said.

Tsurumi-sensei laid out the pen and paper for my first attempts at writing Japanese by imitating her. All the strokes were written left to right. I tried my best to replicate her writing. It was terribly difficult. The stroke sequences were intended for right-handed individuals. I was left-handed and so I would smear the character I had just attempted as I drew my left hand across it. I was making strokes in the direction opposite to what was natural for me, so I tried making the characters as a left-hander would. Tsurumi-sensei saw immediately what I was up to and corrected me.

"Do them just as I do them."

"But I'm left-handed," I said.

"Nevertheless, your characters will look slightly different if you make them that way. You must make right-handed strokes . . . like everyone else."

"How will I ever learn to be a great calligrapher?" I said, teasing.

Tsurumi-sensei said the most famous calligraphy was not always readable. Some of the greatest had been done by artists when they were drunk. Thus, they created abstract shapes that vaguely resembled characters which they themselves were unlikely to recognize when sober.

Tsurumi-sensei came three times every week and each time one of my co-workers was detailed to escort me to the same room. It was uncomfortably like being in grade school, when you couldn't leave the room without being accompanied by a monitor. One was kept track of.

Tsurumi-sensei rarely offered explanations for grammatical rules, usually because she had not analyzed the situation herself. I could see the benefits of such an approach. Word selection is not usually that conscious a process in conversation, so having to apply rules to generate a sentence is a hindrance. It was helpful to have whole phrases and sentences actually memorized, as she had instructed. Yet it was a hard, even painful method difficult for adult students.

Often I would have no clue as to the meaning of a phrase I was parroting. Nor did I know how to use it. Even if I said it fifty times, I was no closer to understanding it, just as a *kanji* character, copied in perfect stroke order, still conveyed no information to me. Clearly it was no coincidence that *manabu,* "to learn," was so close to *manebu,* "to imitate."

The textbook was odd as well. Its vocabulary was fairly impractical and useless. Also, I was being taught "formal" Japanese, which meant I would be able to address anyone without fear of offending because I had been insufficiently polite, but I wasn't learning the colloquial language that was being spoken in the office or on the street.

I wanted to ask Tsurumi-sensei why things were said the way they were, and asked her to teach me the words for "why" and "how." They were difficult to use, she said, and deferred the question. Frustrated, I asked if there was some way, other than rote memorization, that I could be taught. Memorizing without comprehending, I argued, seemed futile.

She looked astonished, if not aghast. Recovering herself, she continued with the lesson.

That afternoon I got a phone call at work from Tsurumi-sensei's boss at the language school. "I am sorry that you are unhappy with your teacher and wish a replacement," she said. "Tsurumi-sensei reported that you criticized her teaching methods and often asked 'why.' Our students usually do as their teachers tell them. However, I will assign you a new instructor, of course."

I declined the offer and assured her that Tsurumi-sensei was a very good teacher, and at the next session I made it clear that I wasn't criticizing her. She seemed to grasp what I was trying to say and even agreed to give me some explanations if I would try to do as the textbook directed, without constantly asking her "how" and "why." In a phone conversation with an old grad school friend from Tokyo, I mentioned my problem with writing characters left-handed and the comments and near ridicule my left-handedness had occasionally provoked. I asked how Japanese lefties managed. There basically were no left-handed Japanese, he said, only maybe 2 or 3 percent of the population. From childhood on, all children used their right hand. Left-handedness was unacceptable and not permitted.

•

Lunch was always with the same group, who all had precisely the same dish every day: noodles. I asked one of my group why. He said, "We like noodles."

The group worked together, met together, and ate together. Many company employees even ate dinner in the Sony cafeteria, especially those who had to work overtime or lived in the dormitory or in homes without cooking facilities. Consequently, company cafeterias and small local restaurants were regularly patronized. Homes and apartments might have a single burner; almost none had ovens, I was told.

Everyone, I noticed, kept the same lunch partners day in and day out. Each table defined a group. Women sat at separate tables. The times I tried to edge away, to make new acquaintances, I was quickly herded back.

So I ate with the same men I had eaten lunch with since my first day. They took their meals the same way they took their work: seriously. At 11:10 I would join the lines of gray uniforms that ascended to the cafeteria. By 11:35 we would be seated; by

11:45, when I was just getting to the best part of my meal, I'd look up and see four empty bowls, their silent owners staring at me, waiting. As I bolted my food, to keep from straining their patience further, I could see they were chafing to get back to their desks.

The only alternative to luncheon conversation (which was not forthcoming) was to watch the large television screens mounted above the tables. Usually they showed advertisements for new products, bulletins of company news, and the taped encouragements of Sony's chairman, Akio Morita. I looked at the faces of my lunch companions fixed on the TV overhead and resolved to try some new people. Why not the women on my team? They seemed friendly, and it was easier to understand them. The men swallowed their words and had a guttural delivery that was hard to decipher. Besides, it would be a nice change.

The next day I invited Imai-san, the most outgoing of the women, to lunch. She was so shocked she was speechless. After stammering, and with obvious hesitancy, she finally agreed to have lunch in the cafeteria and we returned to our workstations.

At lunchtime I found her in the cafeteria surrounded by three other women. As I approached, her friends giggled and bowed their heads to avoid meeting my eyes. They peered instead at Imai-san as if to say, How did you get into such a mess?

"So where do you live?" I asked Imai-san.

"Yokohama," she said and fell silent.

"That must be a long train ride, is it not?"

"Yes." More silence.

"What do you like to do on weekends?"

"Shop."

There was another uncomfortable pause. While I labored to make conversation, the others watched and listened closely, anxiously. They looked as if they were hoping that I wouldn't ask them anything. Why were they so nervous? Was it because I was American? Because I didn't speak too well? Or were they just shy?

Despite the difficult lunch, I was not deterred and kept asking women to lunch, only to get the same shocked reaction each time. Finally, Takagi-san took me aside.

"At Sony, men eat only with men, women only with women. It is an unstated social rule. You are upsetting the social balance by doing this new thing."

"I see."

"Furthermore, everyone has lunch partners and eats with those partners every day. You are welcome at your group's table but not at the other tables. If you disturb the arrangement, you will invite nasty comments and disrespect from others. Please try to avoid becoming 'a nail that sticks out.'"

" 'A nail that sticks out'?"

"That's right," Takagi-san said. It was a very Japanese proverb. "The nail that sticks out gets hammered."

It was the first time I heard this saying. Where I had grown up the most common one was "The squeaky wheel gets the grease," but I got the point. Tsurumi-sensei had already taught me that the Japanese word for "different" could also mean "wrong."

FOUR

LOST IN SPACE

J took up chatting with a vengeance and even managed to have a simple conversation with Sato-san, the young woman who sat behind me. To my surprise and delight, at the end of our conversation she invited me to visit her family in Yokohama. But, of course, she never raised the subject again. It was an invitation proffered out of politeness. Politeness required that I, in turn, thank her and forget about it.

As my conversational skills increased, I found that often I would start a sentence only to be interrupted by the person I was addressing. They're not very patient, I would think and I'd stop speaking. Only they would, too, and there would be dead silence.

The times they initiated a conversation their sentences seemed curiously punctuated. Although I waited to hear them out, they never seemed to finish a thought. The longer they spoke, the more hesitant they seemed to get. Sentences were left dangling; it was maddening.

Every other sentence seemed to end with a question: "Ne?"

"Right?" It eventually dawned on me that the appropriate response was, "Soo desu ne." "Yes, it's true."

I also began to add the hesitant *ne* to my assertions, and to reply with *soo desu ne* to observations made to me. Thus I slowly learned *aizuchi,* the little words and phrases that aided the flow of conversation in Japanese.

The speaker expects a listener to occasionally interject an *aizuchi,* such as: "I see . . . I hear you." "Is that so?" "Right." This is to show involvement. Hearing an *aizuchi* word interrupting him, the speaker knows the other person is attentive and listening. Not being interrupted makes the speaker think the listener isn't following or is upset.

One morning, Takagai-san answered the phone and turned to me, saying, "This telephone call is for you, but . . ."

" 'But' what?" I said.

" 'But' . . . it is just a word. 'But.' It's what you say at the end of a sentence so as not to sound too . . . too . . ." He faltered. "To give balance," he said, finally, and I understood.

It was like "probably," another word I often heard at the end of a declaration. Questions put to me were similarly fuzzed. People would pose a question: "Do you want a cup of tea?" Then add, "Or something?" Or else they would say, "Would you like a cookie . . . more or less?"

Naru, the verb "to become," was similarly common—that is, things rarely happened due to cause and effect. Instead, they would just "become." Nohara-san would never say, "I didn't get my work done so I had to stay late and work overtime." He would say, "Overtime became necessary." It was no one's fault; it just happened: It became necessary.

These were all small ambiguous expressions that allowed others to participate. They were invitations to partake that made communication a group endeavor. Their ambiguity also robbed sentences of any possible aggressive tenor, rendering them curiously oblique, and their passive construction made it seem as if no one person was ever solely responsible.

I understood perfectly as I discussed with several co-workers some simple office arrangements. Bits and pieces of a sentence would be supplied by three or four people. It was as if everyone was finishing the sentence for the other person, only to have someone else pick up the sentence and continue. The group was speaking. The group was harmonious; the speakers, content.

●

I was feeling homesick for the sound of an American voice so I decided to call one of the three other Luce Scholars, Joel, a third-year medical student who had won a year's internship at a Tokyo hospital. Despite the strict ban on personal phone calls in the office, I decided to risk it and dialed his work number.

The hospital operator said, "Moshi-moshi."

I answered, "Moshi-moshi," and drew breath to continue, but she said, "Moshi-moshi," again. I didn't know what to do and was silent a moment.

"Moshi-moshi," she said. "Moshi-moshi," I replied, only to hear her answer, "Moshi-moshi."

Just as I was about to hang up, Takagi-san whispered, "Say, 'Hai' the next time. I did and finally reached Joel and arranged to meet him for dinner.

I picked a neighborhood restaurant I had chanced upon my first week at Sony, when I had wandered about, starving, while trying to find a place to eat. Joel laughed at my recollection of poking my head into one place that turned out to be a mah-jongg parlor filled with loud voices and clacking tiles, then walking into a place that was obviously a restaurant, with pictures and plastic models of sushi in its window. That one turned out to be a fish market. Finally I had stumbled onto the small establishment where we now dined. My first time there I had pointed to plastic food models outside in the window, as I couldn't read characters then. I had been the only customer and the proprietress had been extremely friendly and helpful, as she was tonight, coming over to inquire after my friend and to welcome us in the typically homey fashion of local restaurants. Like the other patrons, I was a regular, part of the group, and the owner was wonderfully welcoming and kind.

The other attraction were the prices. The food was simple, primarily rice with flavorings, the common fare of middle-class Japanese, but it was substantial and filling, and cheap. Joel was impressed, too. We paid our bill without having to worry about the tip as there was neither tipping nor any tax on individual meals costing less than $20. The Luce Foundation paid us almost $1000 per month, and we all budgeted carefully. The money was ample for me, given my dormitory rent, but prices in Tokyo could be sobering if one ordered the wrong thing, like melon. Melon at a produce stand cost $28 apiece. A fixed price meal in a first-rate restaurant could easily run $400 per person.

We wanted to talk more after our meal and went to a *kissaten,* a modern teahouse, for dessert. There were magazines, newspapers, music, and coffee for $2 a cup. Over cakes and coffee, we compared notes. Unlike my arrangement, Joel was living with a Japanese family, the Nishiyamas, the parents of Taro, a visiting medical student he had met at Yale. He liked them a lot, but they were getting to him.

"Last week they wouldn't let me out of the bathroom. I had been in the shower about five minutes and was drying off, when Mrs. Nishiyama called through the door to tell me I hadn't taken long enough. To make sure I was clean, I should get back in for five minutes more. So I turned the water on and let it run while I shaved. Then, another morning, I came downstairs early, about six-thirty, and this awful smell, like pizza, hits me. Mrs. Nishiyama had gotten up early to prepare breakfast specially for me, something she knew I'd like, something really American." Joel grimaced. "Spaghetti and meatballs! I had to eat this huge vat before I could get out of the house, and it was scarcely light. God, I wish I were in a dormitory so I could have some freedom."

"Wish again," I said, and described my living arrangements.

Each morning I flipped the little marker in the dormitory foyer that indicated whether I was in or out, and Hashimoto-san wished me good-bye. I responded with the ritual, "I am going and will come back." When I returned in the evening I would say, "I am home now," and Hashimoto-san would say, "Welcome home." Whenever anyone entered or left the dormitory, a bell sounded to alert him of each arrival and departure. He always kept track of you.

Dorm hours were strict. Each night the gate closed at ten. To get in after that, you had to crawl through a low, swinging subgate, like a pet through a pet doorway. Anyone going away overnight had to sign out and state where he was going, the address, the phone number, and the length of his time away.

Only Sony employees were allowed inside. Any outsider had to be received in a decrepit lounge by the front door. Women were not allowed inside at all. And it was the same way at the company offices. I had asked Kamakura-san, my team's assistant manager, if the other Luce Scholars could visit to see what my workplace was like. "Sure," he said, "they're welcome to visit and can stay up to five minutes."

He wasn't being sarcastic. Even businesspeople who came to

Sony to negotiate agreements, or on other business, were met in the lobby and conducted their meeting at tables right there, by the threshold. Only insiders could come in. Outsiders were not welcome in any facility. Sometimes, I said, I wondered if I was even excluded to some degree for not being entirely "in."

Joel nodded, unsurprised by these revelations. The Japanese, he thought, tended to draw strict lines between private and public. They rarely entertained at home, he thought, the customary meeting place being outside, at a restaurant or teahouse. What with two-thirds of Tokyo housing not hooked up to sewer lines, and with housing so scarce and living space so small, it seemed a bit like Paris, where one's social life was conducted in public places. He also thought they were extremely isolated as a society. Any number of times at the geriatric hospital, when he was making Grand Rounds, a patient would awaken and loudly exclaim "Gaijin!" and point at him in wonder. Many older Japanese simply had never seen a Westerner before. Yet his fellow doctors bristled when he persisted in expressing his interest in Eastern medicine. His exasperated Japanese supervisor had finally exclaimed, "Japan is *not* the East!"

The teahouse was closing, even though it was only 10:30. We hadn't had enough contact to last us, so we decided to risk the wrath of Hashimoto-san and go back to my dorm, which was nearby.

We made it inside all right, sneaking in like a couple of kids, and we continued our long talk, mostly about what we were experiencing. We got around to the Japanese proclivity for avoiding anything direct. I said that when I asked my co-workers whether they thought decisions I had made were good or bad, they would never say. At most, they would use a shortened form of a negative phrase to avoid actually saying the word—that would simply be too blunt.

Joel had certainly run into this, too. A good many patients at the hospital were terminally ill with cancer, yet no one ever seemed to die of it. Rather than upset a patient by telling him he had cancer, doctors purposely withheld such information and gave much less grave diagnoses. Usually it was something far less serious and probably curable. Even the patient's family might not be told. When the patient died, it was commonly attributed to old age: natural causes.

To Americans, it would be unthinkable for a doctor to with-hold a diagnosis in this manner. In Japan, not only was it expected, it was desired. A patient did not need to know his diagnosis or prognosis—that was the doctor's domain. The patient simply trusted the doctor to do what was best for him.

We had run out of time. Joel had to run to catch the last train, but when I opened the door to peer down the hall, there was Hashimoto-san, standing in the hall, chatting with one of the other boarders. Why he was up so late, I didn't know, yet there he was, talking endlessly. He wouldn't stop.

Nervous about the train, Joel said, "What the heck," and suddenly made for the window. He was halfway out the small opening before I could say anything.

"Wait," I said, but he was too preoccupied with struggling to get the rest of himself through.

"Who would have thought I'd wind up climbing out a dormi-tory window at my age—and a boy's dorm, too. If this ever gets out . . . what a fix for a Jewish American prince. I'm going to tell all in my memoirs when I get back." He grunted with the effort of squeezing himself out the window. "*A JAP in Japan* I'm going to call it."

"Come back," I said. "It's not much of a drop to the ground, but then there's a seven-foot wall you'll never get over."

"Oh," he said, and stopped struggling, then slipped back into the room. "So what do we do?"

With time running out, I went outside and distracted Hashimoto-san with questions about some bills while Joel slipped past and made a successful getaway out the front door, the bell sounding as he exited.

Hashimoto-san paused in our conversation, listening. The miniature door in the gate wheezed open and then shut. "What was that?" he asked.

"What?" I said. "I didn't hear anything. The wind perhaps."

He broke off our discussion of my bills and stepped farther out into the hall foyer. I smiled to myself and turned away.

Returning to my room, I vaguely sensed something was missing. Then I remembered. Earlier I had borrowed a chair from a vacant room. I had done so without asking. Without asking, Hashimoto-san had borrowed it back.

●

Back in graduate school I had had two great friends, both from Tokyo, where we all found ourselves now. I called them up and made a date to meet. When Hashimoto-san heard that I was going out into the city, he insisted on personally showing me the best way to Shinagawa Station. Knowing how easy it was to get lost, I actually took notes along the way so I would be able to find my way back at the end of the evening. I made it to the station fine. It was surrounded by bicycle stands full of bicycles of the old-fashioned fat-tired variety long abandoned in the States in favor of the sleek multigeared types introduced from Europe. In Japan, the sturdy, fat-tired fifties models were preferred.

The train arrived promptly and brought me to my destination exactly on time. It was great to see my pals again, although a little strange. I had gotten so used to their American personas that it was mildly odd to see them in their native setting. They had "become" Japanese again, slightly different, more relaxed, more confident. In school, in Los Angeles, they had constantly asked questions about American culture. Now the roles were reversed; I was the outsider with all the questions.

Before I realized it, it was past midnight and Tokyo's transit system had stopped operating. I had missed the last train and the only alternative was a cab. Cabs in Tokyo were expensive, with a $3 charge just to get in. Also, I had been warned that finding a cab was particularly difficult for foreigners. Tokyo cabbies were notorious for refusing Occidentals because they wished to avoid the inevitable misunderstandings and embarrassing difficulties in communicating destinations. Taking leave of my friends, I went out into the chilly night air and raised my hand at the curbside. I expected to wait a while, but three cabs sped right over to me, competing for my business.

Doors popped open automatically. I got into the nearest Mitsubishi and showed the driver the card Hashimoto-san had given me with the address of the dormitory. The driver grunted and we took off. After a short ride, we pulled up in front of Shinagawa Station, and he made it clear this was the end of the line for me. As he could not be dissuaded, I paid him the extravagant amount on the meter, which sent him into a cold rage. He showed *me* a card that said there was a surcharge for rides after midnight. After a long exchange, I realized what his displeasure was about. It seems the way to hail a cab after midnight was to hold up your fingers, each finger indicating the multiples of the meter charge one was willing to pay. Without realizing what I was doing, I had held up my whole hand. Unhappily, the driver eventually accepted less, for the simple reason that I did not have the money to pay five times the fare. Clunking his door closed, automatically, he whooshed off. Now all I had to do was find my way home, using the notes I had taken.

I walked down the main street, retracing my steps, and started up the hill toward the Sony dorm. Except that after a while things looked unfamiliar. Thinking I had missed a turn, I doubled back, only to find another store with an identical sliding door, indistinguishable from the first. I turned up the collar of my jacket and concluded I was lost. It was 1:30 and disturbingly quiet in this back neighborhood somewhere in Tokyo where I stood alone in the dark.

A pair of revelers came tottering past. I asked in miserable Japanese for help. They looked at my card and nodded sagely, as if I were on the right path, yet I clearly wasn't getting anywhere after a few more futile sorties.

An hour later someone turned up who spoke English. He read my card, too, but said he wasn't exactly sure where the address on the card was located. Why not, I wondered. The address was clearly written in Japanese.

"Most streets in Japan," he said, "don't have names. Nor are buildings on a street numbered consecutively."

"No?"

"No. They are numbered according to when they were built."

"Chronologically?"

"Yes, exactly. The first building erected is Number One, the next Number Two, and so on. The top line of your address card, here, says Japan." He pointed, I nodded, confident I was in Japan. "This is the prefecture—the state. Next, the city and *ku*—borough—and then the *chome* or district. Finally, *bancho,* the neighborhood. And that is it."

"That's it?

"Hai."

I puffed my cheeks like a squirrel. No wonder so many address cards had a sketchy map on them detailing landmarks and occasional street names.

With typical Japanese courtesy, the English-speaking gentleman escorted me to a *koban,* a police sentry box, where, with the help of the neighborhood patrolman (who meticulously noted all the details of my plight for his log) and his map, I was eventually returned to the threshold of the Sony dorm. It was 3:30 in the morning. I thanked my guide profusely and waited until he was out of sight before I crawled through the after-hours gate.

●

Interoffice memos drove me crazy. So did the papers and articles routed to me for my edification. The information in all of them seemed to appear in haphazard order, in whatever sequence the thoughts occurred to the writer. Each small section might make sense, but the relationship between sections seemed arbitrary at best, and were usually nonexistent. There was no logical progression, no argument offered in a coherent sequence. Obviously, the writers deemed the order in which the information was conveyed as being unimportant so long as all the pieces were there.

Where Westerners expected information presented in orderly fashion, the Japanese seemed willing to wait patiently until all the information was laid out in whatever order, then assimilate and process the bits and pieces until they made sense. They seemed to look upon written information like a jigsaw puzzle whose various pieces they examined somewhat simultaneously. The order in which they received the information seemed to matter not at all. They almost seemed to deal with it three dimensionally. Certainly, there was nothing linear about it, no beginnings or ends, just muddled middles, and it drove me to distraction.

Every time I was given travel directions, I was reminded of this graphic or visual inclination of theirs, as opposed to the orientations I was used to. I was used to cities laid out in a pattern, with streets laid out in a grid or some other discernible scheme, with streets designated by name or number, with buildings sequentially identifiable. It seemed to me that the citizens of Tokyo could call up visual images of their streets with near total recall as to all landmarks. Instead of names and topographic directions, or points of intersection, the Japanese oriented and guided themselves by visual recollections of physical features. It was like dealing with Eskimos.

I was often told to meet someone near a certain statue of a dog, or under a certain restaurant's neon sign. Streets would be referred to by their dominant edifice. I would be told to look for a friend "on the McDonald's side" of the street. The relationships between places was what mattered, even in the instance of maps.

Japanese maps, in fact, did not even always show distances drawn to scale. Nor was north automatically to be presumed the primary point of orientation. Sometimes north was on the bottom, sometimes on top, or not given at all. The trick was to think of the map's contents as a group. The relationships within the group were accurate, but the group's relation to the outside world was ambiguous. Such information was not viewed as critical.

It was this other psychology or mindset that I contemplated when an invitation came for me to attend a meeting of Sony's English Club. I was delighted to accept as I hoped to meet a lot more English-speaking employees all at once and perhaps even find one of them who would be willing to have me work for him, as I seemed to be stuck doing next to nothing where I was.

The club turned out to have about twenty members who met once a week after work. It was their aim to improve their reading and writing skills. We sat around a large table in the company's clubs facility, with the senior person occupying the customary place of prominence at the center of the table, opposite the door.

The meeting opened with several of the men reading aloud from their business memos. I listened attentively as the first businessman, then the second, and then the third read their memoranda. They read in incomprehensible syllables that I took to be some kind of technical or scientific Japanese because I couldn't understand a word. Slowly it became evident that these memos had been written by Japanese employees of Sony posted in the States. The memos had been sent back to headquarters in Tokyo, where we sat, and were being read—in English—as models to be imitated by the club members.

To say that most were grammatically incorrect would have been the grossest understatement. They were, in fact, unfathomable, incomprehensible—in a word: gibberish. Nor could one have gotten past the bizarre accent in which they were being read. The deadpan renditions of these memos, done with utmost seriousness, were just a travesty. You couldn't understand what in the hell these men were saying. Yet the club members seemed to have no difficulty following the baffling sentences.

What was going on? I strained to listen more closely, thinking that perhaps they were using English hybrids, as was their want. The Japanese love to use English abbreviations: one could order "L," "M," or "S" packets of "friedpotato" at fast-food emporiums, for instance. They also had a weakness for borrowing English words, transforming them, and then reincorporating the strangely scrambled words into everyday usage. *Gohan,* for instance, was Japanese for rice eaten from the traditional bowl with chopsticks. Eaten Western style on a plate with a fork, it became *raisu.* Similarly, a word processor became a *wah pro;* a PC or personal computer became a *pasa con;* the baseball player who patrolled between second base and third was the *shorto;* and the game they played was *besubaru,* broadcast to fans over *radjo* and *terebi.*

Maybe it was their notorious problem in pronunciation of foreign languages, as theirs had the fewest number of distinct sounds of any major language. Their tendency to combine *l*s, *r*s, and *d*s into a single consonant was well known, as I had again seen the other night on an English-language news show when a reporter interviewing the American First Lady asked her about the upcoming "presidential erections." Yet for some reason, as if this problem did not exist, the Japanese named their products things like Tercel, Cressida, Cellica, Corrolla—names almost unpronounceable by Japanese. Or else they would come up with business names like National and Technics. These were pronounced locally as Na sho na ru and Te ku neek tsu.

After the fourth reader finished his interpretation, my comments were solicited. I broke out in a cold sweat. A swirl of realizations alighted in my poor brain. It was not mispronunciation I was listening to, or specific bastardized words. These people were speaking some other language. But how and what?

All Japanese students, I knew, studied English for six years. However, they did not study it in order to speak it; their only goal was to pass the national college entrance examinations. Since native English speakers were not allowed to teach in Japanese public schools, all were taught English by other Japanese. A handful of instructors may have lived or studied abroad, and perhaps had better pronunciation and more natural usage skills, but most spoke with heavy accents and in stilted English derived from outmoded textbooks. The students memorized long lists of vocabulary, replete with archaic expressions, and studied elaborate rules of syntax divorced from all context. Hour after hour they imitated their teachers' pronunciation, and the end result was this—some incredible closed linguistic system.

All, I realized sitting there, had thoroughly mastered this non-English and could understand each other. What observations might I make, perhaps? the senior person wanted to know.

My stomach tumbling—cornered—I told them the truth: what they had been reading aloud bore almost no relationship to English as spoken and written by native English speakers.

Eyes blinked but remained steady, faces remained impassive. It took a few moments for my comment to be addressed. Perhaps they had mistaken my simple Japanese, or they could not believe I had meant what I said. But my words did at last penetrate enough to provoke a cold indignation. My opinion was brushed aside. It was implied that I didn't know what I was talking about. We moved on to pronunciation practice.

I was treated to some odd utterances, only faintly related to my native tongue. Prevailed upon to correct their speech, I did so, only to be told my pronunciation was mistaken; my corrections, errors. They were speaking correctly; they had to be, because they had no trouble understanding one another. I would not, I had the distinct impression, be invited back to the English Club.

That night, back at the dorm, I called my Japanese friend from graduate school. I described to her my experience at the Sony English Club and enumerated my fearful conjectures about the teaching of English in Japanese public schools.

"Oh, yeah," she said, matter-of-factly. "It's called 'Japlish.'"

FIVE

A HARD DAY'S NIGHT

A two-day weekend was coming up and I was desperate to get away. An ad in the *Japan Times* had piqued my curiosity. It offered a weekend retreat that consisted of an introduction to Zen Buddhism. I was intrigued enough to sign up.

Fifteen of us met at the railroad station on Saturday morning and boarded the train for Jojo-in. There were ten Westerners and five Asians. The group was evenly divided in gender. Looking out at the countryside, the dirt roads and timeless hamlets, it amazed me how rural most of Japan remained. But then the feudal system had only ended a little over one hundred years ago.

The Jojo-in Temple was in Higashi Matsuyama in the mountains, so I had brought warm clothing. But while it was brisk when we detrained, the air was clean and fragrant. When we reached the temple, the program commenced without ceremony. A monk taught us the mechanical aspects of Zen meditation and told us not to think, to completely clear our minds. We were told not to try to have no thoughts; instead, we were to allow our minds to clear.

A fellow meditator asked me how many times I had "sat *zazen*" and I sensed this was not going to be a leisurely introduction for novices. Clearly some of these "beginners" were well versed in Zen and had come to enjoy a long weekend of meditation.

We went right to the meditation room, where we were told to remove our shoes and socks and to sit on the plump black pillows facing the blank wall. Our legs were supposed to rest on the tatami-covered floor, in either the full-lotus or half-lotus positions. I could not twist my legs into the full-lotus configuration, so I settled for the amply painful half-lotus. When everyone was ready, the lights were turned off and the session began.

We had been told to breathe slowly and deeply, to sit motionless with our spines straight. Above all we were not to think of nothing. Rather, we were simply not to think. The room was dark and silent, except for a monk who patrolled in a slow, deliberate shuffle. His task: to observe and correct. He examined each meditator carefully, checking that the form was proper, spines straight as rods. When anyone got fidgety, started swaying, or shifted into an incorrect posture, the monk's job was to "help." This he did with a sharp whack across the errant meditator's shoulders. The tool he used was a bamboo stick. The stinging slash was not intended as punishment, but only to remind one that one's body and mind were wandering, and that greater discipline was necessary.

Courtesy seemed to require that the monk give you a warning tap on the shoulder before he disciplined you, presumably so that you could prepare yourself for the help you were about to receive. I wasn't completely convinced that the warning was benevolent; the seconds of anticipation between the tap and the blow were sheer agony, but the tap did let you get your ear out of the way.

Ten minutes passed without anyone receiving correction. Then someone obviously tired. The sound of the monk's shuffle ceased. We heard the whiplike crack of the stick on someone's tender flesh and a controlled but anguished cry. I couldn't see anyone else as I dared not turn my face from the blank wall, but I and the thirteen others cringed. After that my concentration was split between the long shadow of the wandering monk, which periodically crossed the wall before my half-closed eyes, and the desire to sit immobile.

Before long my legs started cramping. The pretzel position I had assumed was cutting off my circulation. The dull cramp turned painful, and then hardened into an excruciating knot, but I didn't budge. My leg went numb. I wondered whether I would ever walk again and waited anxiously for the triangle's sound that would signal the half-hour. Finally, finally, it chimed.

When I tried to get up, I couldn't. I had to use my hands to unfold my legs and after that it was several minutes before I could confirm their existence. It was even longer before I had enough sensation to be able to walk, and two more hours of evening meditation still awaited us.

We were assigned an hour of cleaning and gardening, activities that required action but not the application of the conscious mind. Dinner followed. It was a silent vegetarian affair. We had just enough time to swallow some pickles, mountain vegetables, and two bowls of brown rice. Not a word was spoken during the meal, as silence allowed a person to fully concentrate on his food. As I had forgotten the necessary gesture to indicate that I had had my fill of rice, the server piled on more rice,

higher and higher. My bowl rivaled Mt. Fuji. Since all participants at Zen meals must finish when the leader does, I stuffed
my face to keep up with him.

There was no dessert. Instead, we wiped our dishes clean
with hot water and a pickle slice, then placed them in a cloth,
which we tied with the proper technique so they would be ready
for the next meal. I wanted to ask for direction but I couldn't;
Zen etiquette forbade participants to pose questions.

Dinner over, we returned to the *zazen* chamber for extended
meditation. The pain from the earlier session had barely faded. I
asked the leader if I might withdraw during the session if it hurt
too much.

"No," she said. "If you cannot do it, then do not join us at
all."

I decided to give it a try. The half-lotus was as painful as
before but less numbing. Also, part way through the session we
were directed to rise to our feet, and there ensued a trance-walk
by candlelight, round and round the room. During this eerie,
dreamy procession, we followed one another in a circle, feet
bare and eyes half closed. We chanted as we circled, ever so
slowly, to a solemn rhythmic drumbeat. This was designed for
us to achieve a different consciousness from that achieved in
seated meditation. It also broke the monotony. By 9:00 P.M. we
were finished, by 9:10 P.M. lights were doused in the communal
sleeping room.

Moments later a bell clanged in the darkness. I groped for my
watch. It was ten minutes to four. Without any chance even to
wash up, we were called from our exhausted slumber and
marshalled by candlelight in the damp and chilly darkness. A
triangle chime sounded. It was *zazen* time again.

Sitting there half-asleep, my bare feet freezing in the cold
mountain air, I concentrated all my being on not nodding off so

as to avoid the rude awakening I would have experienced if I had. Then it was 5:00 A.M.—time for more Zen cleaning and sweeping. Six o'clock, breakfast—a rerun of last night's silent repast, except this time we were served the leftovers from the night before.

The Zen weekend was almost over. Refreshed by our experience, we would return to our stressful urban lives. I could hardly wait. Before we departed, however, our leaders gathered us together for a lecture. For two hours they explained why there had been no explanations. Their absence, they said, was as important to the Zen experience as the activities themselves. Zen emphasized experiential apprehension, not intellectual comprehension. Explanation—analysis—was not only superfluous but actually interfered with a person's ineffable ability to experience.

One of the female leaders said something interesting: that to a Japanese the stomach, or *hara,* is the emotional center, the role Westerners assign to the heart. In meditating, one breathed deeply, from the belly, from one's spiritual middle.

It was a much weightier concept than "gut feeling." The belly, it occurred to me, was the target in seppuku, ritual suicide, quite different from the head or the heart a Westerner would target as the primary places of one's being. This fit perfectly with what she was saying about the location of one's spiritual and physical centrality in the *hara.* And then she said something that really struck me. She said a most important element in Japanese conversations was not what was actually said but what was communicated "belly to belly." *Haragei,* "belly talk," depended as much on what was not said as what was. *Haragei* was the way one conveyed strong feelings, when articulating them would diminish their depth and be too direct.

Ritual, a sense of form and order, and the development of

patience and acceptance, she said, were also integral to Zen. Our leader extolled the virtues of patience and suffering in achieving Nirvana, and then we were all treated to one last helping of *zazen* before heading home.

•

A s a foreigner residing in Japan I was required to register with the authorities and receive an identity card to be carried on my person at all times. On Thursday afternoon I decided the moment had come to take care of this chore.

The Tokyo train and subway lines acted as a grid by which the various neighborhoods and sections of the city could be roughly defined. Since the Yamanote train line made a ring around the city's center, it was possible to describe locations as either within or without this circle. Likewise, the Chuo Line served to demarcate the northern metropolitan sectors from the southern. The government office I had to go to was in southeast Tokyo, about halfway between Sony and the financial district. With surprisingly little trouble, I found the office building and presented myself for registration.

In the waiting line with me were many Asians and I struck up a conversation with the man just ahead of me. He was, he said, Korean. His family had been in Japan since 1909, when thousands of other Koreans had been forcibly brought here by the Japanese military to work. Min, Korea's last queen, had been executed earlier by the Japanese, her body burned, and her countrymen conscripted to labor for Japan, while the king found sanctuary in the Russian embassy. More conscripts followed after Korea's annexation in 1910 (perhaps a million in all) and many more during World War II. Their descendants totaled about 700,000 Koreans resident in Japan. One of his ancient ancestors, an architect, had been among those who designed and built goodly portions of such cities as Osaka, Kyoto, Kobe, and Nara using Chinese techniques, a fact the Japanese were loathe to acknowledge. They did not like to be reminded, he said, of their militaristic imperialism or of Korean architectural contributions.

Had the family reemigrated to Korea, I asked. No, no. His family had been in Japan now for several generations. I nodded politely but I was puzzled and formulated another question in my basic Japanese. How was it, I asked, that he was waiting to be fingerprinted and registered as an alien if his parents and he had all been born here. He looked faintly bemused. *Gaijin,* the Japanese word for "foreigner," he explained, did not simply mean newcomers from other lands. Nor did it mean strangers. Literally, *gaijin* meant "outside people."

It is just as it is in a group situation. There is *uchi,* things inside the group, and *soto,* that which is outside. "You and I," he said, switching to English, "are *gaijin.* We shall always be *soto*— outside."

●

Afterward, I wandered through the autumnal afternoon. God, Tokyo was immense. Most neighborhoods were bursting, every structure jostling every other for every last centimeter of space.

The buildings were not attractive. The city had been rebuilt quickly after the war, with little regard for aesthetics. Only the brightly colored roof tiles enlivened the drab white and gray combinations the Japanese seemed to prefer. Many of the cars were white, I noticed, and nearly all the women wore gray, their red lipstick pronounced. White-gloved policemen struggled with the traffic snarls at the larger intersections, directing drivers with military precision. Everything seemed to be white, gray, white, with the occasional dab of red from tail-lights or lips. The traffic light beeped, alerting the visually impaired to the flow of vehicles.

I passed an electronics store that had every kind of Sony product I had ever heard of and several I'd never seen in the States. Remembering my own Walkman, I put the tiny ear-phones on and switched to FM radio, forgetting that there were only a few FM radio stations in Japan. The FM bands were allotted to television stations for the transmission of the audio portions of programs. I switched to AM.

Toward evening I ambled into a commercial strip alive with neon signs, most in English advertising Japanese products, stores, and restaurants. Franchised American fast-food em-poriums, imitation American fast-food shops, and native-snack kiosks abounded, as did magazine stands, each filled with Jap-anese magazines, many bearing English names. I stood outside a sushi go-round and stared unabashedly at the little plates of raw fish skimming past the patrons seated at the counter, car-ried along on a rotating belt. Two doors down was a pizza parlor offering slices with a variety of toppings, including squid and pineapple.

Bicycles stacked high with boxes of ordered-out food ca-reened around corners at sharp angles; motorbikes, too, their wooden *obento* boxes held in place by an elastic *bungi* cord and centrifugal force. Something reminded me of my very first meal in Tokyo. The four of us went out that first night in Japan: Joel, Ken, Ann, and I. We had gone to a nearby bar for a bite. The proprietor received us regally and boasted about the great American golfers he had played with, showing us trophies from the tournaments he had won, describing the fancy American cars he owned and the prominent Americans he had met. The Japanese were fanatical about golf and baseball. The tiny sticks of chicken, pickles, and beer had come to 20,000 yen—$80! We were astonished. With great bravado, he cut the bill in half.

The temperature was dropping but it was still pleasant. Everyone taking the night air seemed to be wearing something with something in English slashed across it, however inappropriate or even senseless the words might be, just so long as it was English and the sound of the words was appealing to the ear. Live Beer . . . Happy Hunting Summer . . . the way something sounded was everything. Why were they such Americophiles?

I stopped to admire a kid's bicycle in a shop window. It was fire-engine red and beautifully built. The trademark read Miki House. Next door a men's clothing store displayed button-down-collar shirts in a wide range of colors, yet each pink, blue, yellow, and green pile was identified as "White Shirts."

A woman in kimono and obi waited at the corner for the traffic light. A group of youths sat at a counter eating: bright red pickled ginger, sun-yellow radishes, green horseradish, black-seaweed-wrapped sushi rolls. I recognized McDonald's golden arches across the street but not the name emblazoned across it: Makudonarudo. A young boy tugged at his mother toward them, loudly pleading, "Ham baa gaa, ham baa gaa!"

I passed small stores selling fast food, sweets, and snacks of every variety, and magazine stalls with a blinding array of periodicals, many of them with mystifying English titles and Japanese text, such as *Pia, Hot Dog, Focus, Big Tomorrow. Popeye* was the leading men's magazine, much followed by my colleagues in expanding their wardrobes. But the most popular magazines of all were the illustrated adult comic books called *manga.* The ones for women were like soap operas; the men's *manga,* however, were a bizarre mix of caricatured violence, nasty sex, and heroic adventure. Their range of subject matter was enormous: There was even a *manga* on physics. The bookshops were likewise jammed with titles and browsers. The Japanese read omnivorously, more per capita than any other nation.

Vending machines were everywhere. Ticket vending machines for the trains and subways. Sake vending machines. *Pachinko* machines offering the hypnotic Japanese version of pinball. Battery vending machines to fuel the portable televisions, radios, tape players, calculators, hair dryers, flashlights, walkie-talkies, CD players. There was even a condom vending machine.

A beer dispenser ejected cans in various sizes, from the common eight-ounce to a three-liter keg that looked like a small barrel. And everywhere stood soft drink machines. One offered a blue-and-white can with an imitation Coca-Cola design. It was a Japanese version of Gatorade. The label, in English, read Pocari Sweat.

●

The capstone to my in-house briefings on Sony was a field trip to the manufacturing facility at Atsugi. I was delighted at the chance to see for myself the company's pristine and highly regarded plant, especially as we (five journalists and an equal number of junketing businessmen) were to be given a VIP tour by a knowledgeable staff member.

The plant lived up to its impressive reputation. It was, for one thing, gigantic, the size of a convention center. Inside, running all the way around the huge interior area, was a glassed-in observation walkway. Even to enter this, we had to put on immaculate white gowns and caps and put on sterile slippers, then pass through a special room into the encased walkway.

Beyond the glass, inside the facility itself, were thousands of workers covered from head to foot in sterile white outfits and goggles. Each was bent to the eyepiece of a microscope, peering at the inner works of a microchip, the heart of the recent electronic revolution.

To get into the sealed central work area, each employee stripped, took the required chemical shower, entered a clean room and donned specially treated caps, long-sleeved shirts, gloves, mouth masks, and even goggles that prevented any foreign matter originating in the eyes from entering the sterile atmosphere of the innermost work area. Looking at the precautions being taken, you would have said it was living matter they were working with. It was said by experts to be the cleanest environment on the planet.

The reason for the fantastic precautions was the absolute cleanliness required to manufacture the microchip. Impurities were intolerable to its electronic physiology.

The sight of this plant and its workers was truly impressive. The tour was not. No matter what I or the others taking the tour asked, the guide's answers were evasive.

"How many microchips are produced here every day?"

"Many."

"What sort of techniques are employed in their manufacture?"

"State of the art."

"Is gallium arsenide the chief element?"

"Ostensibly."

"Is the technology still licensed from Intel and Texas Instruments?"

"I am sorry, I don't understand the question. We must move on now, please."

Returning to Tokyo, I sought out Takagi-san and spoke to him about my situation in the office. He had been introduced to me as my liaison in the division, my English-speaking go-between. I understood now that he was my *senpai,* my immediate superior in the hierarchy—my senior. It was to Takagi-san that I communicated my frustrations about the role I had been assigned. He, in turn, would advise me, his junior, instruct me by example, and report the situation to the assistant manager, if necessary. Only the assistant manager was allowed to speak to the manager, and only the manager spoke to the general manager, Murata-bucho.

It was a system and a structure that had not appeared on the organization charts I had been shown, which enumerated relatively few levels. But it was the daily reality within the company, and I was observing its unwritten strictures in speaking to Takagi-san.

I was, I explained, terribly frustrated. I had yet to do a stitch of computer-related work, or real work of any sort, since I had arrived. Certainly, I had had no opportunity for hands-on experience in Japanese management. I was still far from the fluency needed to understand technical manuals or follow the exchanges I would overhear in the Computer Division. I did not explain that I now knew that American employees in the company had come in technically well trained and fluent, or else knew no Japanese and performed menial work.

There was no way I was going to learn Japanese in the time permitted. Would it not be advisable to place me elsewhere in the firm where language was not a problem?

Takagi-san listened to my grievance in perfect silence. I thanked him for his time and left.

Every day that I came to work, I checked with Takagi-san and did whatever he asked me to. Despite his terse style and reserved character, we had developed a rapport. As the weeks passed, however, I sensed something was wrong. Takagi-san, the star of our team who always did his work well, began to come in late, appearing at the gate after 8:30. I cringed at first, expecting that he would be fetched by the boss and escorted to his desk, the shaming procedure I had been told by personnel was the norm, but it thankfully never happened (neither was anyone ever chastised over the public-address system for forgetting to set location cards).

Takagi-san's behavior evinced discontent, even defeat. I was amazed and worried. He was a top graduate of Tokyo University, the Harvard of Japan, with a reputation as a brilliant abstract mathematician. He went to work at Sony right out of college, first as a trainee, of course, then as a programmer in the Computer Division. He had been a programmer for six years and had mastered the job years earlier. He wanted to move on, to assume tasks better suited to his intellectual abilities, but he couldn't. Promotions were accorded by seniority, so his might not come for five years, or seven, or even another ten.

He was a *sarariman,* a "salaryman," and could not seek a better position elsewhere. It simply wasn't done, nor was it probably attainable, as another company was unlikely to hire him anyway. No firm would take on someone who had left another's employ because of dissatisfaction — or, really, any other reason — and one was self-evidently dissatisfied if one wished to leave a position. Few *sararimen* even attempted to change jobs for this reason, and those who did, merely by making the attempt, were labeled as peculiar. The conventional thinking was that if an employee was prepared to leave one firm, he might well be disposed to leave another, making him untrustworthy.

Nor could one hide previous employment. Your *rirekisho*, or "work history," was dutifully maintained by your employer, and (although denied) managements would certainly avail other firms of the contents of such files.

The only alternatives available to an unhappy employee were to seek out a small company or business, or to go into business for himself. Neither avenue provided prestige or security, nor the same level of monetary reward as a large firm.

The system allegedly offered stability and certitude, and eliminated the stress of competition. It also eliminated the need for regular review and formal evaluation, thereby avoiding potential conflict and maintaining *wa*, "social harmony." However, Takagi-san did not seem at all so confident of his future or content with his career. Although single, he dreaded the overseas tour Sony would require of him within the next few years. He just did not want to leave Japan and his family, yet it would probably be asked of him, and he would have to accept if he was to keep hoping for a job upgrade or advancement.

It began to dawn on me that the man I had complained to about my inherently temporary dilemma was facing a built-in, permanent one with a lifetime guarantee, and I began to see variations of Takagi-san's mute unhappiness in the situations of other workers around me.

A good *sarariman* worked long hours, constantly. Overtime was a way of life and one of the first words I had learned at Sony: *zangyo*. Much of it was counterproductive, if not downright silly. Wives actually worried if their husbands came home too early. Rather than embarrass her with the neighbors, spouses followed the work-overtime-play ritual by putting in the obligatory overtime and spending the rest of the evening eating and cavorting with their colleagues. Starting around ten each evening the *sararimen* began staggering homeward.

Nohara-san admitted to me privately that he would be coming to work the next Saturday not because he had anything to finish but simply to "show his face," thereby demonstrating his commitment and support to those who were legitimately there. I questioned the efficacy of so much extra work done over so many hours. Why was it a constant?

One reason seemed to be the standards set for them. Often they were impossibly high. Since failure would mean a terrible loss of face, failure was unacceptable. Seeing the world in Zen black and white, they considered anything less than 100 percent as completely inadequate. It was like being in a nation of perfectionists, and the overall goals were set by managers who had grown up in merciless postwar poverty and remained obsessed with the need to survive through arduous work, even though the reality had obviously changed. Excessive work and absurd hours were not just virtuous, they were a mindlessly worshiped fetish.

Procedures and policies were rigid, arbitrary, and usually doubled the time necessary to complete assigned tasks. The physical work conditions were wearing. The place was noisy, crowded, and messy, and made everything hard. The work itself was usually boring, which made it tedious. Even the group meetings, held every Friday after lunch, were in reality boring, compulsory, and mostly useless exercises. No one really listened. Yet not to attend would have been a grievous transgression, so everyone showed up, bowed formally to the boss, and sat there, bored. I saw no evidence of the enthusiasm Western reporters and writers extolled as a major factor underlying Japan's economic success.

There weren't nearly enough secretaries and assistants, and there was insufficient rest. The buzzer would sound at 5:30, officially ending the paid workday, yet usually no one would react. They would just keep on working, right through their dinnertime. Most stayed until 7:00 P.M., "finishing what needed to be done." They went home late and exhausted, night after night.

Often, it seemed to me, they would have been better off stopping and taking up their tasks again the next day, fresh instead of fatigued. But they couldn't. Management pressure had created a peer pressure that had become self-perpetuating. Respect was accorded by co-workers and supervisors to those who worked long hours. The more hours, the more praise.

Similarly, normal vacations of two and three weeks, to which my colleagues were entitled, were almost never taken. The implication was that one's contribution was important to the group. He or she could not responsibly take more than two or three days at a time. Such self-indulgence would increase the burden of the other team members. Likewise, sick days were theoretically available but were taken only when someone was gravely ill. Usually, workers came in with bad colds, fevers, flu, whatever. Not surprisingly, this resulted in near-epidemic illness in our claustrophobic, humid office during several weeks of the winter season. And a whole office of sick people was not productive, which meant—more overtime! Even the rare national holiday did not constitute totally free time. Invariably, everyone had to come in the following weekend to make up for the lost time. Takagi-san actually said it one day: "Overtime itself breeds more overtime."

The one way in which Sony favorably differed from other companies was that Sony employees worked Saturdays only occasionally. In most firms, employees put in the extra day as a matter of course. Recently, the government had actually recognized the physical and psychological toll of this national workaholism and was encouraging businesses to cut back hours. The necessity of the six-day, sixty-hour week, it argued, was over; the postwar economy had been rebuilt.

The bureau set up to promote this concept was called the Office of Not Working on Saturday. According to the papers, the bureau was not having much success despite a valiant effort. The staff was working day and night, six days a week.

SIX

PHOTO OPPORTUNITY

ince my professional interest in Japan was thwarted for the time being, I decided to take up social life with a vengeance and partake of group life at the office. Instead of begging off when invited out by office-mates, I accepted. There were welcoming dinners and going away dinners and impromptu dinners of the whole team. In between, I spent several evenings a week out, drinking and eating with other team members on these less formal occasions. I became like my neighbors, returning to the dorm only to bathe and sleep.

The dinners were held at a variety of restaurants, and all were elaborate and delicious—also very expensive, often costing each of us $35 or more. And every week there was some event. I was going broke. How did my colleagues manage? It also bothered me that there was so little conversation at these gatherings. Being together seemed to be the chief idea. Talk was almost superfluous.

There was even a weekend disco party. We were an unlikely mix of workers and middle managers as we headed for the disco with the unlikely name of Radio City. Had anyone ever heard of the New York City theater of the same name? No, no one had. As we entered, my teammates headed for a corner. Everyone encouraged me to dance first and I finally complied, but I felt a little odd to be the only one of our group out on the floor. Finally someone confessed that they had just wanted to watch an American do it. I forced a smile and gathered my courage to ask someone to dance.

Japanese conversations were more about feeling out the other person than two people stating what they thought, felt, or wanted. As you never asked anyone's preference directly, I rehearsed beforehand my question and its appropriately vague coda: "or something?" Then I asked a young lady if she would like to dance, or something. She refused. So did another. Imai-san filled me in.

"We don't dance with one person," she said. "We dance with our group."

"You're kidding."

She wasn't. The entire crew strode onto the dance floor. Lights pulsated in time to Michael Jackson. The whole group was dancing. There were hundreds of people in the place and no one was dancing with anyone else. Everybody faced the center of the circular dance floor and a blinking, flashing electronic totem. Everybody there was part of a group, gyrating in proximity to everyone else.

The nights we went drinking, no women came. *Akachochin* were not for women. *Akachochin* meant "red-lantern place." Most were wood paneled and decorated with tawdry posters and knickknacks of all sorts, often cats beckoning with one paw. The preferred drinks were beer and whiskey, wine and sake being somewhat unmanly. If the place served hard liquor, a customer could buy an expensive bottle and then store it at the bar. These were called "keep places." Japanese whiskey was expensive and tasted awful but had status. It was also a quick way to get drunk. Again, the costs were considerable, perhaps $25 on the average. One week I was invited to join the group every single night. The bars were noisy and it was hard to hear what little was said, especially since we mostly sat facing the same way along the bar. Nohara-san said I wasn't missing much. Conversation was not that important, anyway; being together, sharing the evening, was the primary objective.

Customers seated at the tables, I noticed, always avoided placing themselves directly across from one another. Sitting face-to-face was too confrontational. Sitting at ninety-degree angles to each other spared them from looking directly at their companions.

In addition to socializing with colleagues, I undertook to stay in contact with my fellow Luce Scholars, seeing them as often as possible at *kissaten* (teahouses) and staying in touch by phone. The latter was surprisingly difficult.

Like all Japanese businesses, Sony made it clear that the office telephone was not for personal business, and I dared not transgress too often. This left me with my only alternative: pay phones.

Phone service was inexpensive—a three-minute call was 10 yen (under a dime). It was also confusing. The pay phone would warn that my time was up. I would deposit more money and then I would be promptly cut off. No matter how much I deposited, this scenario kept repeating and I kept getting cut off. Maybe this was why the Japanese were so terse, I thought. Three minutes was all they were allotted per call.

Nohara-san explained. It was necessary to first put in lots of 10-yen coins. The unused portion of the deposit would be returned when the call was completed. Simple. Except the telephones were color coded according to the type of service they provided. There were red, blue, yellow, green, and pink phones. Most often in street booths the phones were blue and yellow. Public places, shops, and restaurants usually had red, pink, and green instruments.

Blue phones, or red ones with gold bands, could be used for calls longer than three minutes in duration. However, red phones only accepted from one to six 10-yen coins. Blue ones accepted up to ten 10-yen coins. Yellow phones were the most desirable. They could be used to make any kind of call and even accepted 100-yen coins. The only catch was they didn't return any change. The pink and green phones—I stopped right there to get an aspirin and never did find out about pink and green phones.

Most of the time I tried to make my calls from the dormitory pay phones, especially the yellow one on my floor. There was no privacy but in the early evening the hall was usually quiet. One night I had been talking with Joel for nearly twenty minutes when Hashimoto-san came bustling out of his office toward me, making cutting motions across his neck.

"Too long! Too long!" he called out.

I hung up and inquired what was the matter.

"Your calls are too long, too long. The limit is ten minutes. That is the rule."

My head swiveled. There were two other pay phones, neither one in use as there was no one around. But I did not even bother to protest. Rules were rules.

Having gotten a little bored with my noisy evenings out with the team, I thought I would try going out with just one person, maybe to a quiet restaurant or teahouse where I could hear and perhaps comprehend the other person. I decided to experiment by asking one of my female co-workers to go for coffee after work. Kaneko-san was extroverted; she might accept, I thought.

I asked her if we could talk over coffee after work. "But what would we talk about?" she said. I said something obvious—work, films—and she eventually agreed. Later in the afternoon, however, she stopped by my desk to say she couldn't. She was coming down with a cold. "Unfortunately, it requires the cancellation of our appointment." We postponed it for a week. On the appointed evening, Kaneko-san joined me for coffee, but with three or four other teammates she had invited along. When I asked for another coffee date, she accepted. But a week later she canceled again: a dying grandparent. The next several appointments were likewise canceled. I tried asking other women in the office. Each had an elaborate excuse: It was not possible on that day, circumstances existed that precluded such an event. Sensing some social prohibition, I telephoned Joel and Ken and asked them if they had run into anything like this with female acquaintances. Neither had, which surprised me. Heck, maybe it was me. (Impossible!)

Kamakura-san took me aside in the office. "Some of the women," he said, "have asked me to speak to you. They request that you stop asking them to go out for coffee. It embarrasses them. In fact, some of them are very angry with you. They can't understand why you don't get their message."

I was stunned. "What message?"

"Don't you know, if a man and woman are seen together outside of work, everyone in the office assumes they are having an affair, that they are . . . sleeping together. For this reason no woman here will go out with you."

I was mortified and apologized profusely, yet I did not fully accept what I had heard. Something did not add up. Could so anachronistic a view of contact between male and female co-workers really be the rule? At my next Japanese lesson, I asked Tsurumi-sensei about the warning Kamakura-san had given me.

She scoffed at what I had been told. "A frog that lives in a well thinks his well is the whole world. People at Sony don't know how the rest of the world behaves. They are a peculiar bunch. They even walk differently from the people who work at other companies."

I had sensed the situation correctly. This stricture was peculiar to Sony. I was understanding Japan better. My shoes came off automatically now when I entered a house, I could identify a post office by the "T" sign out front, I went up stairways on the left-hand side. My so-called work was boring but my social engagements were many. At least they were during the week. Weekends were rougher. On weekends, co-workers went home, and the dorm cleared out.

When another two-day weekend approached, I made plans to visit Nikko, the ancient home of a shogun, located about ninety miles from Tokyo. Checking the schedules, I saw that the speediest train offered "Romance Cars." Why not, I thought. But when I purchased my ticket from a vending machine and tried to board, a female attendant in white gloves stopped me. "I am sorry. This train is full."

"When is the next one?" I asked.

"In forty-five minutes . . . but it is full also."

"Is there one after that?"

"I am so sorry . . ."

"But why?"

"All the Romance Car trains to Nikko are booked for the weekend. They were sold out long ago. We Japanese can only travel on weekends and holidays, so the trains are always very crowded then. The regular train also goes to Nikko, but it takes a bit longer."

"How long?" I said.

"About four and one half hours."

I nodded. That was twice as long. The holiday-starved Japanese had reserved every seat, probably on every special train in the country. The station attendant excused herself and I considered my options. Maybe I would stay in Tokyo after all. However, the woman returned, smiling.

"Sir, I spoke to my superior and we have found you a cancellation. But you must hurry. The train departs in less than a minute."

"Fabulous." I thanked her and ran, and just managed to get aboard as the train pulled out. The cars were packed but, yes, there was my empty seat, waiting. Quite soon we were out in the countryside, zooming past rice fields, each full of little cones of cut rice, drying in the sun.

I was startled to find that the toilet facilities even on the train were of the Japanese ceramic-hole variety. How did people manage on moving vehicles, especially the elderly and overweight. Judging from the grip bars and the button alongside to summon assistance, perhaps my trepidations were not baseless.

In two hours I was far from Tokyo and Sony, in one of the most beautiful places in Japan. At least everyone said so. Actually, it was hard to know for sure; it was impossible to see anything because Nikko was so crowded with sightseers. The crowds were dense, hopelessly overwhelming in size and numbers. It was hard even to walk. Loudspeakers blared descriptions of every temple and shrine, however, reminding the throngs that what they were milling around—had they been able to see it—was extremely beautiful.

Now I knew what they meant when they said Japan was crowded. Obvious remedies, like flexible work schedules or even staggered hours, were unacceptable: some people would be off when others worked. The implicit differentiation was unthinkable. After a while I gave up and sat down on a bench to rest. The crowds surged past with no letup. Sitting there, I saw that the mass of sightseers was really a collection of tour groups, each led by a young lady in immaculate uniform and bonnet, hands covered by spotless white gloves. Each guide held aloft a big banner with the group's name and number, and, through her megaphone, called, "Kochira e dozo! (This way, please!)" as she confidently herded her flock along. "Kochira e dozo!"

To ensure that no group member strayed off or got lost, everyone wore a little pin bearing his or her name and the name of the tour group. The travelers may have been lifelong co-workers, old schoolmates, or simple tourists who had shared only an hour or two with one another. No matter. Each group climbed up into bleachers in orderly ranks, held a signboard, and stood together to pose for a group picture.

Leaving Nikko, I went on to Lake Chuzenji, a small hot-spring resort. I was tired and I wanted a comfortable place to stay overnight. As I inquired at the *ryokan* (inns) and *minshuku* (family-run guest houses), a disconcerting pattern developed. Each innkeeper cheerfully showed me various rooms and asked how many there would be in my party, or where my family was. When I said that I was alone, a puzzled, then disapproving look appeared on their faces. Each time I was told either that all the rooms were full or that they didn't let rooms to single travelers. Finally, it was getting late. One of the guest-house proprietors wavered and consented to give me a room. I leapt at it.

Curiously, the proprietor kept checking up on me. I got tired of his peering at me and went out for a walk. As in Nikko, I was hardly alone. The mobs of guests from the various inns were all parading through the rustic streets in cotton robes emblazoned with the name and crest of their hostelries. I promenaded along with the prevailing current of robed tourists and returned to my room.

It was amazingly cold inside and there was no heat; I retired quickly and covered up. During the night the temperature dropped below freezing. I piled the futon blankets on but, of course, my head protruded and it was now so cold that I could see my breath.

Sleep was impossible. I got up and searched the closet for more to wrap myself in. What I found was a kind of nightcap that looked like a masked hat. The instructions were beyond me but I put it on, gratefully. It covered my head nicely, also my face, as there was a transparent plastic face piece. I lay down again, but the cap was uncomfortable. After a short time, the nightcap became so warm that I started sweating. The face piece fogged up, and then I had trouble breathing. I kept adjusting the cap and passed a miserable night. The next day I was relieved to get back to Tokyo.

Monday morning, during the tea break, I recounted my adventure to my office-mates. Maruyama-san and the rest were obviously amused by the tale of my unusual weekend.

"That wasn't a hat," she said with a laugh. "That was a fire mask. It's supposed to prevent smoke inhalation in case of a fire emergency." Everyone had a good laugh.

More privately, I asked her why the innkeepers had denied me a room. Was it economics? Did they want more paying guests per room?

"Oh, no," she said. "No doubt they were afraid. In Japan, people who travel alone are thought to be terribly odd."

"How so?"

"Persons who rent single accommodations in mountain areas like Chuzenji often do so because they are intending to commit suicide. Normal people, Gary-san, always travel in groups."

•

Joel's host family, the Nishiyamas, invited the three other Luce Scholars for Sunday night dinner at their home. I was really looking forward to it, not having yet been inside a Japanese home. This was an opportunity not often accorded *gaijin,* even by exceptionally welcoming families like the Nishiyamas. I wanted to see Ann and Ken, too, and hear about their experiences in Japan, and I was especially curious to meet Mrs. Nishiyama, my first Japanese Jewish-mother. A housewife with a will of iron, she managed her home, her children's educations, and taught in a cooking school: a formidable woman, I knew.

So, it couldn't be put off any longer: I had to get a hair cut. So many people at Sony had admired my curly hair and asked where I had gotten my "perm," that I was getting self-conscious. They weren't teasing about the permanent. Curly hair looks Western and stylish to Japanese and an increasing number of women, and even men, were getting their straight black hair "done." I did not relish the attention paid to me because of my now long wavy locks, and I made an early Saturday appointment at an international hotel's barbershop on the theory that they'd have some experience coiffing foreigners.

Arriving at the appointed hour, the first attendant greeted me and seated me, offered me cigarettes, and wrapped my face in a hot steamy towel. All service required attentiveness, but a personal service, like a haircut, required special attentiveness. It was practically a point of honor in Japan. A second attendant, an extremely beautiful woman, approached, lightly placed her hands on my shoulders, and, in an intimate tone, asked me what I'd like. She was the barber.

Before I could describe the Katzenstein Look, she started cutting. I explained the shape and length I preferred, even as she worked. She said, "Hai, hai." The scissors flashed. When she had finished, I put on my glasses and wished I hadn't. She could have worked for the Marine Corps. I now looked like every one else in Japan.

I paid my bill and went on to Takashimaya in Ginza, one of the finest department stores in the country. The generous sign over the entrance was in English. It was not yet open so I strolled around the area. Passing parked cars, I stopped to admire their craftsmanship and happened to notice the names of the Japanese models: Bluebird, Accord, Civic, and a woman's car named Fair Lady.

A small crowd had gathered around three *buriko:* teen-aged girl singers without much talent but who were *kawaii*—immensely cute. Cute counted for a lot in Japan, whether koalas, Mickey Mouse, or cloying kid singers. Cuteness and youth were an irresistible combination, it seemed. It started to rain and I put up my umbrella.

At precisely 10:00 A.M. the department store's front doors were opened by a bevy of attractive girls in neat, crisp uniforms. They bowed deeply and chorused "Good morning" and "Welcome." A young woman helped sheath my umbrella in a special plastic covering provided by the store. Free baby-sitting was also available to customers. I strolled to the escalator and was greeted by a lady who thanked me for coming. I hopped onto the moving stairs and smiled back at my benefactor. The very-proper-looking, matronly woman in front of me was carrying a large shopping bag with huge lettering and graphics on it. The lettering read *Marijuana,* and beneath it was an identifying picture of the plant and an abbreviated user's guide. At the top of the escalator stood more than a hundred employees awaiting customers; all were facing me. As I came off the escalator they all bowed and welcomed me.

Bowing is obligation in action. A person greeted with a bow must bow in return. It is simple politeness. Of course, the original bowers must bow again to acknowledge the other's bow. Needless to say, the recipient of the first bow would be rude if he did not bow in kind, so down I went, and, naturally, they bowed again. A marathon was under way, I sensed, and finding a convenient ending point was not so easy. One had to keep an eye out to see if another round was in order, while maintaining a low enough posture long enough to express the proper respect. Some department stores, I knew, even sold bow meters, electronic yardsticks that helped the neophyte bower learn proper angle and timing.

The key to the grand finale was to find the moment when both parties came up simultaneously, so that neither was obligated to go down again. Given the laws of probability and a hundred and one bowers bowing at one another, I realized this could take a while. Bowing yet again, I bobbed toward the next leg of escalator stairs and slipped aboard, then ascended, still bowing, the hundred people below raising their faces higher and higher with each dip as I was borne aloft, the odd angle proving a challenge to the rules of bowing etiquette.

With some relief, I turned as I approached the next floor, and got off, only to find another clutch of employees dipping down. I bowed deeply and remained bent over, not daring to rise for fear they would see my face.

Extricating myself gracefully, I bowed away down the aisle. At the watch counter three sales girls appeared. Each took part in assisting me to purchase an inexpensive wristwatch. I looked for a house present for the Nishiayamas but could not decide on anything and opted for the elevator down to avoid a repetition of the mandatory bowing on the way out. The elevator operator, a woman in a pastel uniform with matching hat and white gloves bowed. Speaking in the exaggerated servility and flowery delivery of the ultraformal *keigo* form, she announced each stop of the automatic elevator in a lilting falsetto. She was there to push the buttons and, like the other staff, to demonstrate the store's great appreciation of our patronage.

I got off and wandered. The department store was vast, with endless aisles and counters at which to buy designer perfumes, designer clothing, designer anything. Brand-name liquors, brand-name pens. I picked up a Gucci bag to see what it might cost and was surprised by the low price. I looked closer. The bag was an imitation but that did not seem to matter, judging from the frenzy of buying. Imitation or not, it satisfied the Japanese consumer's boundless desire for readily identifiable brands.

Mostly the prices were sky high. Japan's multitiered middleman distribution system ensured work for countless thousands who added nothing to the product except the expense of their salary. It was the price paid for employment of vast numbers who would not otherwise have work. As a result, a Sony radio cost more in Tokyo than in New York. So did everything else.

I worked my way down to the basement, where I found an incredible array of foods unlike anything I had ever seen. There were mountains of every kind of edible, some of it freshly preserved atop shaved ice, all gorgeously displayed and exorbitantly priced. I bought two little dumplings, which I intended to eat on the spot, but the girl behind the counter insisted that she had to wrap them. The wrapping was typically elaborate. Two different papers encased the dumplings and the object was put into a bag; the bag was then taped shut and the package given a twist that made it into a small work of art. I shouldn't have been surprised. Everything, from a cookie to a painting, came exquisitely wrapped, especially gifts. Presentation was all. If the form was inappropriate, the contents would be irrelevant. Thoroughly intimidated, I gave up my search for a house gift.

On Sunday evening I set out for the Nishiyamas. The house was a small, detached, two-story structure on a comfortable street lined mostly with two- and three-family homes. A freestanding single-family house, like theirs, was rare. Between their doorway and the street was a narrow, fenced-in strip of grass tended with obvious care. It offset a kidney-shaped pond the size of a large puddle. From the shoes at the door, I could see that Ken and Ann had already arrived. I added my shoes to theirs and knocked. Mrs. Nishiyama greeted me and took the flowers I proferred, then led me into the living room. It was tiny by Western standards but contained all the furnishings you might expect in a formal living room. It even had a baby grand piano. What with Mr. and Mrs. Nishiyama, their son Taro, Joel, Ken, Ann, and myself all occupying the room, it was no wonder it seemed crowded. In the empty space of the special alcove, called the *tokonoma*, was a beautiful floral arrangement. In schoolboy Japanese, I complimented Mrs. Nishiyama on her ikebana. My hostess said, "My, your Japanese is good."

Mr. Nishiyama, not to be outdone, insisted on speaking English to us, although I could tell he had trouble understanding Joel or me. But Ken, who used half sentences and short phrases, had no trouble making himself plainly understood.

Dinner was announced and we wedged into the dining area. Mrs. Nishiyama plied us with huge quantities of seaweed, rice, and fish for sushi rolls, which we could make ourselves. It was delicious, but as soon as we finished our helpings, Mrs. Nishiyama piled more food on our plates. She was very animated and not to be refused. Besides, rejecting additional helpings would have been the height of rudeness. We smiled and ate everything on our plates, as custom required. Before, during, and after dinner, Mr. Nishiyama snapped photos of us from every conceivable angle. I blinked away the latest camera flash and spoke to Ann briefly.

She was enjoying her work in an architectural-design firm but was living in a tiny one-room flat in the busy Roppongi District and hoping to move. The elevated expressway passed right by her window and made it impossible to sleep decently, or to get any fresh air. Ken, who was working for a parliamentarian, said he was still in the rented room he had found over a rice-cracker shop. Maybe the dorm wasn't so bad after all.

Officially replete, we were ushered into the living room once again. Two clarinet cases were set out on the piano; young Taro and Joel were going to play a duet. Somehow it came to light that I, too, played clarinet. Taro rushed to a closet and produced a third instrument.

The three of us played woodwind trios as Mr. Nishiyama recorded the event with his 35mm camera. Then I did a medley of original compositions for piano, to the accompaniment of more camera flashes.

Quite sated, we took our leave. A few days later a stack of photos arrived from Mr. Nishiyama, copies of all the snapshots commemorating our dinner and concert. Joel called and said we had been a great success and would be invited back soon.

SEVEN

DIMED

A s in all Japanese companies, women at Sony were not hired for real jobs, nor were most educated for them. It was assumed that work for them was a mere interval between schooling and marriage. They were therefore given minimal training, minimal pay, and minimal challenges. Out of a total staff of 130 people in the Computer Division, four women had four-year college educations. Most had associate degrees in home economics, which were deemed more than sufficient training for their chief task of programming, this being an increasingly formulaic endeavor, a white-collar assembly-line job. As long as the steps were strictly followed, like a recipe, one could write a program.

In my idle hours—too many of them—I would practice my Japanese by conversing with the women on my team. Unlike the men, they were open to idle talk, their accents much easier, and they were lots better to look at. Most of them openly said that they were just marking time until they got married and got out. They were expected to wed by twenty-six. If, like Kaneko-san, a woman reached twenty-six and was unmarried, she was called "Christmas cake," because after her twenty-fifth birthday she would be like a stale holiday confection that no one would want.

Unlike the men, the women at Sony had few illusions about fulfilling professional ambitions. Although more than a quarter of the country's college graduates were women, Sony and the other companies gave them less responsibility and lower pay, even for doing the same jobs men do for considerably higher pay. Men received more; it was just an accepted social norm.

At an afternoon tea break I thought I'd shake things up in the tiniest way. I served the tea and snacks. My co-workers fell silent, brows furrowed. The normally chatty break was suddenly quiet. Everyone managed thank yous as I served, but they were all obviously taken aback. I even got a semiprivate scolding from the female colleague whose turn it was to serve. She said, "You don't need to do such work. Pouring tea is a girl's obligation." She was in her twenties and a graduate of Keio University, one of Japan's finest private universities.

Many women in the company worked as Office Ladies, or OLs as they were commonly called. OLs were receptionists and clerks. They welcomed visitors, poured tea, answered the phones. They smiled and bowed a lot. One, whom I got to know, had convinced herself it was important work. It had taken considerable time, she said, to master the intricacies of when and how deeply to bow, to learn the nuances of pouring tea.

Most women in the firm coped by deemphasizing work and emphasizing their interests outside. Tennis was one such activity, pursued with almost as much enthusiasm as was golf by the men. Shopping, however, was the major pastime. The chatter about bargains and labels was incessant. Everyone carried imitation Vuiton bags, Gucci wallets and gloves, wore

Pierre Cardin coats, Norma Kamali dresses, Shiseido makeup. Living at home as they did, the women in the office were able to save and buy tremendous quantities of expensive outfits. Even on Saturday nights, daunting throngs of almost identically dressed women would flow across the broad intersections of Tokyo hot on the trail of goods and good times. In Shibuya, Shinjuku, Roppongi, and the other entertainment districts, the movie theaters, restaurants, bars, discos, and streets were filled with young, stylishly dressed women out on the town in small groups.

●

With my master's degree in computer science, it was not my ambition to become a programmer. It was not what I had come all the way to Japan to master. Yet, as a Sony trainee, I seemed to have no choice. I was scheduled to learn the Sony method of COBOL computer programming, which I had already worked with in the States. Resigned to my fate, I sat through several lectures delivered in Japanese by my female colleagues, who of course knew it best. I could only follow about a quarter of what they said in Japanese, so I could not even learn to program in Sony COBOL. To my further chagrin, I was the recipient of the ladies' commiseration. They did not seem able to distinguish my linguistic inability from my problems with their programming. It was as if they believed it a skill that was the exclusive province of the more intelligent Nipponese. How much had I understood, they always wanted to know and, typically, always made me quantify my answer, pressing me to tell them some percentage. "Seventy percent?" they would ask, and I would shake my head no. "Forty percent?" No again. "Twenty percent?" Again no. How much then? "Three percent," I would say, and they would cluck and express sympathetic dismay.

Takagi-san, who understood all and was wryly amused, suggested that, until I could follow the technical language of the lectures, I might keep busy by learning to use a Japanese word processor so as to document the programs I would eventually learn to write. (Optimist!) He assigned Maruyama-san to teach me the *wah pro,* or word processor, so that at least it would be fun. I liked her, as he knew.

Maruyama-san explained that the *wah pro* had had a major impact on her work. With about five thousand *kanji* in common use, until the *wah pro,* most everything had to be written out by hand. Because of the multiple strokes comprising the *kanji* characters, the need to reproduce exact stroke sequence made accurate rendering essential. By hand it was time consuming and tedious. The few *kanji* typewriters in existence were large and clumsy to use. The Japanese had a crying need for a word processor, and it was no wonder that they led in developing them, facsimile machines, printers, and computer graphics software.

Sony used the Oasis model word processor, which was quite advanced. It integrated all the possible scripts: *kanji, hiragana, katakana,* and even *romaji,* the Japanese for our roman letters. It was an amazing machine.

To use Oasis, I would type in the sound of the *kanji* character I wanted and the machine would give me a dictionary of all possible characters having that sound, based on the frequency of their use in Japanese, or based on a previous character that had already been used. Depending on the particular character, I might be shown as many as one hundred possible representations.

A hundred?!

As Maruyama-san continued, some of my suppositions were confirmed. She told me that as a student, she had spent countless hours and days memorizing a character's stroke order, definition, pronunciation, and use, all of which one had to master in order to eventually read. Then came *jukugo*—words that combined two or three *kanji* characters. These had to be memorized as well. There were so many that students normally memorized ten new words every school night for each of their thirteen years of basic education.

Japanese students had long terms, starting in April and finishing eleven months later the following March. Using that as one multiple, I tried to calculate the exact number of items I would have to commit to memory but gave up in favor of a rough estimate. Namely, I would have to know at least two thousand to three thousand *kanji* to be able to use Oasis. Up to that moment I had mastered perhaps four hundred. I was going to have problems with the *wah pro*. I smiled wanly. At least I'd get to talk to Maruyama-san. To converse with her was its own reward. She was incredibly patient, her pronunciation crystal clear, and I understood almost everything she tried to tell me about the word processor and *kanji*. This was no mean feat, given the complexity of the written language and the spoken language. Even when I knew what a character meant, I didn't always know how to pronounce it. Each character had one Japanese pronunciation and one or more Chinese pronunciations that had tagged along when the characters had been appropriated. The Japanese pronunciations were generally used when speaking informally, while the Chinese characters—combined in pairs—were used for more formal spoken or written Japanese. So even if I knew what a word meant, because I knew its two Chinese characters, that told me very little about how to pronounce the whole word.

Just to make things even more interesting, a character in word *A* often would be pronounced differently in word *B,* and, for no reason, it would be pronounced differently in word *C.* In effect, there were two sets of pronunciations. And if that didn't give you a headache, there was yet a third set. This was for names, and it was so arbitrary that most Japanese themselves had problems pronouncing the name of someone they had not met and had not heard introduced.

Initially, Maruyama-san's purpose was to teach me to use the *wah pro,* but as the days passed, we spent less and less time on lessons. Mostly we just talked. Maruyama-san, I learned, had gone to junior college where she had studied English and home economics. I was the first American she had ever met. She kept scheduling lessons, but we both knew there was little more that I was capable of assimilating about Oasis.

●

A clock radio arrived in the mail from the States. I thought of recent letters from home. It seemed such a long way in miles and time. I set the clock mechanism to awaken me the next morning, Sunday, when Joel and I had a date for lunch. Then I went to bed.

The next morning I was awakened by the light streaming into my room and the loud sounds of children at play nearby. The clock showed it was only 5:30. I fell back to sleep.

At seven the plaintive recorded cry of a street vendor hawking hot sweet potatoes pierced my sleep. I tried to go back to my dream, but the caw of huge black magpies made it difficult. Still, I managed.

Eventually there was a buzzing sound: the buzzer summoning me to the telephone. I trundled down the hall, wondering who would call me at 8:00 A.M. on a Sunday, but then I had been roused at 2:30 A.M. a few days earlier by friends calling from the States who has miscalculated the time zones. This time it was Joel. Glancing at my watch, I realized it was eleven. So much for the alarm clock radio, I thought, and rushed off to make our date.

That evening I mentioned the odd behavior of the clock radio to my dorm neighbor. He said the mechanism was probably fine; the problem was the difference in Japan's electricity. It resembled common American current but was not identical. Japan's was 100 volts and 50 cycles; America's, 110 volts and 60 cycles. So my American-made equipment would operate at five-sixths the proper speed. My clock, he said, had lost ten minutes every hour since I had plugged it in. Only the eastern half of the country had this problem, he explained, because the American visitors (occupiers, he meant) had installed it. The Western half used German technology and everything worked perfectly. Then he mentioned he was leaving soon.

I hadn't had much contact with him after our first brief encounter. He usually got home late and quickly went to bed — not always alone, I knew, as our paper-thin walls did nothing to muffle the noise either of television or the occasional smuggled-in woman. On weekends he had been away, presumably in Osaka with his family.

"It is time to say good-bye," he said.

I knew he had been only temporarily transferred to Tokyo and said I supposed he would be happy to return home to Osaka.

"I am not going to Osaka," he said. "I will be posted to Saudi Arabia for three years." His tone was entirely matter-of-fact.

"Do you speak Arabic?"

"No, but I will learn."

"Will Sony send you to school for a few months before you go?"

"There is no time. I leave in two weeks."

"When did you find out that you were going?" I said.

"Yesterday."

"That's quick. Your wife will have a lot to do to get ready on such short notice."

"My wife?" He looked surprised. "No, she is eight months' pregnant. She and my daughter will stay in Japan."

"Did Sony know? I mean, that she's about to have a baby?"

"Yes, they know."

"Ah . . . doesn't it bother you? They could have waited until the baby was born."

"It can't be helped. I must do what Sony asks."

Sacrifice was a cornerstone of the Japanese notion of cooperation. I nodded and we said our good-byes. Just as I was about to turn in, there was a sharp rap at my door. I thought it might be my neighbor, but it was Hashimoto-san.

"Didn't you find your rent and dry-cleaning bills in your mailbox?" he demanded.

"Yes, I did. But I cannot pay it until I can get to the bank and get some cash." Practically speaking, there were no such things as checks (or credit cards) in Japan, nor was Hashimoto-san about to accept one of mine. Everything was transacted in cash and I didn't have enough on hand.

Hashimoto-san wasn't buying any of this. "The bill plainly says it is due tomorrow. You must pay me—now. We expect residents to anticipate their expenses. Sony must not be inconvenienced."

Hashimoto-san stood there glaring until, I suppose, he was convinced I really did not have the ready cash.

"As soon as possible," he said, "please," and walked away.

•

Maruyama-san, I realized, had given me half my Japanese vocabulary, and I was most grateful to continue taking lessons from her, ostensibly about the word processor. Quite regularly we worked until the buzzer sounded and then, if Takagi-san and Nohara-san were free, the four of us would go out for a quick dinner, it being understood that she could not go out with me alone.

Like many women at Sony, Maruyama-san lived with her parents. This was company policy for unmarried women. She had no real choice about it and had to commute three hours a day because of it. It was a question of ensuring the company's reputation.

In the afternoon Maruyama-san and I closeted ourselves in the programming area so that she might again instruct me in the Oasis word processor. There wasn't much left to review about functions and disc drives, so we began chatting. Had she ever considered living elsewhere in the world, other than Japan?

"No, no," she said. "I am glad I live where it is safe, where people do not need guns."

"Guns? Do you think Americans need guns?"

"We Japanese read about how Nancy Reagan kept a gun by her bedside for protection in the White House."

"Really?"

"Yes," she said, and paused. "How many guns do you own?"

"I don't own any. Nor do my friends."

She looked incredulous. "But you say you lived in New York. We Japanese all know that New York is very dangerous. Many people are mugged and murdered right in the streets . . . all the time. I've seen it, many times, on TV and in the movies. Also, we have statistics demonstrating that there are ten times as many murders in New York as in Tokyo, even though our population is much larger."

I said, "It isn't nearly so bad."

But Maruyama was insistent: "My friends at Sony of America told me you can't go out after dark in New York City."

We were engrossed and did not sense anyone approaching. Suddenly the assistant manager appeared before us. Kamakura-san said, "Gary-san, do you know how long you have been away from your desk?"

I looked at my watch; it had been nearly two hours. I had not set any location card. There was none for tutoring, anyway.

"Are you really having that much difficulty with the *wah pro?*" Kamakura-san asked.

Maruyama's expression was serious. "Yes, today's problem was very difficult."

Kamakura-san did not seem convinced. "We have work to do," he said. "The lesson was scheduled to be over twenty-four minutes ago. You must not exceed the allotted time."

Maruyama-san said something and scuttled back to her desk, reproved. I withdrew as well, with as much dignity as I could muster. Kamakura-san followed, joined by Takagi-san.

Kamakura-san said, "Are you done with the program yet?"

"Which program is that?" I answered.

"The one on the edge of your desk." He pointed to the sample documentation.

"That?"

"When you were given the assignment last Saturday, you said, 'Yes,' you understood."

"I said, 'Yes,' meaning that I understood what you meant by program documentation, not 'yes,' that an actual program was to be done in one week."

Kamakura-san visibly darkened, I thought. "Does this mean you are not finished?"

Either he had no idea how hard it was to do the assigned task in a strange language, or, once I had said "yes," even inadvertently, I was expected to fulfill the assignment.

"Yes," I said, "yes, I am not finished."

"Ah so desuka," he said, meaning "Oh, I see." He sucked in air as he turned away. Kamakura-san was not pleased.

•

J was summoned to the Asia Foundation a few days later . . . to discuss matters. Mr. Morton offered me a seat in his roomy office, so unusual for Japan.

Sony had complained that my Japanese was not good enough. Mr. Morton's small sigh seemed to imply that had I studied diligently the previous summer, I would not find myself in this fix now. He spoke so decidedly, yet so slowly, that it was hard to correct him. He seemed to assume that Sony was complaining because my skills were subpar for a Luce Scholar. But I knew that conversational Japanese was not the problem. The problem for Sony was that I was not fully fluent. Barring divine intervention, there was no earthly way I could have picked up enough Japanese in the course of a summer's training.

Sony had been very Japanese in voicing their grievance indirectly, instead of complaining to me, and Mr. Morton was being very Japanese in accepting the validity of the company's complaint without hearing out the individual involved. To try to counter this, I offered to converse with Mr. Morton in Japanese, to show him just how much my language skills had improved since we first met. He declined. He had pressing matters to attend to elsewhere and ushered me out before I could say anything more. It was all very oblique and nonconfrontational, and definite.

I went back to the office and into the Personnel Department, to Saito-san.

"Isn't there any possibility of switching to a job where more English is spoken?" I asked.

"We will do our best," he answered, instantly. "Meanwhile, try to work something out with the Computer Division. After all, you are still a trainee."

"But with background and degrees. I am able to do considerably higher level work than the average trainee. But there is little point in trying to learn to write even a simple accounting program in Sony COBOL if I can't even understand the instructions. I mean, I can order food from a printed menu and converse, but it is far from the fluency I would need to understand technical manuals or follow complex instructions. Right now I'm just sitting around. It's unproductive for Sony and a tremendous waste for me."

"We will consider what can be done," he said.

●

I needed a break, to get away from the incessant pressure of doing next to nothing except exhausting myself with the complete concentration required by transacting everything in a foreign language. Although Sony had not scheduled any vacations for me, I assumed a few days off would be no problem. I asked for four days that preceded a three-day weekend; this would coincide perfectly with the visit of Brian, an old friend, and his fiancée, Pat. He was a gynecologist; she, a registered nurse.

Both Takagi-san and Kamakura-san said okay, and conveyed the request up the line to Yoshino-san, my non-English-speaking manager, and he, too, approved it. The second week in November was all mine. I felt as if I had been let out of school.

Brian and Pat arrived as scheduled and we were off to sample the spectacular fall foliage. I made sure that we arrived at the railroad station early. Pat and Brian were curious as to why; they looked puzzled. I explained that I had to peruse presents for all my teammates back at the office, and that this was not some kind of generous extravagance on my part. It was my obligation as a traveler to bring back gifts for all those less fortunate who remained at their desks. In fact, my co-workers had already told me what to bring back for them and, upon my return, they would quickly appear at my workstation to pick them up with hardly a nod or thank you. So I wanted to make sure the shop had the items they had requested.

The gifts were called *omiyage*. Usually they were edible delicacies, and sometimes a handcrafted piece associated with the region the traveler was to visit. I showed them the handy shop, right in Tokyo Station, that carried trinkets, mementos, and special foods from all over Japan, so one did not need to go farther than the station to purchase the requested gifts. Nor did one have to spend any vacation time hunting through local crafts shops and then lugging the stuff around as you toured. You could do it when you got back to town, as I would. Pat and Brian thought this amazing and amusing. Did my colleagues know this is where their exotic requests would be fulfilled? I assured them, yes, they knew. The image of my bringing back gifts from distant places was satisfactory; the reality was conveniently ignored. This was perfectly acceptable.

Aboard the Bullet Train for Kyoto, I felt the weight of weeks fall away. The strain of dealing in another language, the seeming impossibility of gaining access to Sony's inner workings, and perhaps the culture shock of living in Asia had all taken their toll. But now I felt lighthearted and carefree. We sat in our comfortable armchairs, eating snacks and watching the countryside shoot by the windows. A uniformed young girl came down the aisle, looking totally apathetic. In contrast to her rude manner, she praised and proffered to us dried squid in the ultrapolite singsong *keigo* form that sounded like Chaucerian Japanese.

When we stopped at Nagoya Station, Pat asked if the train was on schedule. Without even looking at my watch, I said that this train and all trains—long distance, commuter, even subway—ran exactly on schedule, usually to the second. The schedule was followed no matter what.

As I spoke, I noticed a *gaijin* had hopped out to buy an *obento* lunch box. "Oh, no," I said. Brian and Pat sat up to see what I was referring to. With *obento* in hand and mouth agape, the man watched the train doors slide shut and his bags continue their swift journey to Kyoto while he stood there, bewildered.

"I see what you mean," Pat said.

•

The temples in Kyoto were beautiful—and overrun by the usual mobs of tourists and junior high school students enjoying their traditional school excursions. After a few days, we bused to Takao to see its mountain-perched temples. There, too, the unruly boys were indulging themselves, this time sailing frisbee-size pieces of cardboard across the beautiful valley, ablaze with fall foliage. The Buddhist monk accompanying them looked solemn with his robes and shaved head. But instead of reprimanding them, he joined in, to the boys squealing delight.

In the teahouse at the very edge of the cliff, we chose to sit on the open porch overlooking the valleys and other peaks. Nearby was a couple, sitting side by side, sipping tea and gazing at the mountains. Pat and Brian enthused about the view, the young Japanese couple sat totally silent, sharing the moment, relishing the silence of the *mu,* the "nothingness."

If our conversation had fallen off, I realized Pat and Brian would have felt uncomfortable, the lull would have been a void we would anxiously fill before it became too obvious and embarrassing. The Japanese woman and man were not even facing one another; merely being together and together experiencing the beauty of the moment communicated, even radiated, their harmony and belonging.

Ginkaku-ji Temple was also swarming with junior high and high school students, all chorusing, "Harro, harro. I am a bowee." Stuck for the next line, they quickly called out, "Bye-bye," and quickly rid themselves of the possibility of making a mistake. Like most Japanese, they had an overwhelming fear of committing an error. They would stick to Japanese, especially as they were in a group and loss of face would be magnified.

At Biwa Castle we bought tickets for a cruise of Lake Biwa, Japan's largest, and local sandwiches made of thin white bread (crusts cut off), mayonnaise, and lettuce. As the weather was terrible and no one else was aboard, the captain invited us into the wheelhouse and gave us each a turn steering the vessel. Then he suggested a special outing: the enchanted island at the far side of the lake.

We docked at the island; the captain hopped off and led the way, taking special pains with Pat. He showed us shrines and temples overgrown with vines and weeds, and an ancient cemetery. On a cliff overlooking the water, he asked a favor: to be photographed with Pat in this most spectacular spot. The sun broke through the swirling black clouds at just the right moment.

Back in Kyoto, we decided I would contact the parents of a grad school friend who lived nearby. Mr. and Mrs. Shinoda invited us to dinner at a local restaurant, at which we presented them with a modest gift: a plant. They seemed surprised and commented on the "elaborateness" of the gift.

"Elaborate?" said Brian. "A plant?"

We were invited to a sukiyaki party the following night at their home and accepted. The Shinodas's home was wonderfully typical: Disney posters in the living room, a calendar of half-nude men in the tiny kitchen, and a Buddhist altar in the den. While Mrs. Shinoda prepared the food, Mr. Shinoda showed us into the "reception room." It was a traditional living room, with tatami mats, exquisite screens, wall decorations, and the family's mementos and art treasures. Mr. Shinoda produced two large shopping bags. Each was stuffed with an assortment of elaborately wrapped packages. As he handed each of us a gift, he said, "Tsumaranai mono desu ga."

I translated for Pat: " 'It is a trifle, but . . .' " The last meant ". . . but I hope you will accept."

Mr. Shinoda produced yet more packages. Pat seemed stunned, Brian amused. More packages poured forth, each exquisitely wrapped. I took a quick inventory of mine: an elegant ceramic tea set, fancy green tea, a pen watch, wallet, some socks, a colorful scarf. Pat wanted to know what it was all about. "Obligation," I said. "We gave them a gift." Until the obligation was discharged, the Shinodas would feel the weight of their unbalanced debt.

Brian and Pat received slightly different but equally generous gifts. Theirs were less personal, all except the last. Pat asked me, in a whisper, what they were. I told her: a pair of hand-painted fertility shells.

I had introduced them as a married couple to avoid the problem of their traveling together. In socially conservative Japan, that would not be done. I had also made sure the Shinodas did not pick us up at our hotel, as we never could have explained the three of us sharing the same room, no matter what we concocted. Since most Japanese couples Brian and Pat's age usually had children, the Shinodas were doing their symbolic best to help. It was a warm and caring gesture.

Left somewhat breathless and charmed by all this, Brian and Pat wanted to reciprocate. What, they wanted to know, would be appropriate gifts for their generous hosts. And how had they managed to create such spectacular packages. What was that about?

I tried to explain that the package was crucial. It wasn't the gift or the thought that counted, it was the manner of presentation. The aesthetics of the package were therefore terribly important, as was the brand. Johnny Walker, Black Label, was a highly valued Scotch, for instance, but not Johnny Walker, Red Label. Likewise, Harvey's Bristol Cream might cost as much or more but would probably go to the back of the liquor cabinet. It was a brand whose prestige had not been commonly acknowledged.

What would I recommend they get the Shinodas, they wanted to know. My suggestion was: nothing. It would only set off another round of gift giving. The Shinodas would have to reciprocate with another bunch of presents. My friends resisted but finally gave in. We sent a thank-you note in the best penmanship we could manage and called it a day.

The trip wound down. Brian and Pat said their friend Margo was hoping to come to Japan soon. Certainly they were going to encourage her, given how receptive Japanese were to foreign visitors, how open. They would tell her to look me up. I said the politeness accorded tourists and short-term visitors was one thing. Resident aliens were not accepted as warmly. But sure, Margo could call me.

On the train home, at a stop soon after Kyoto, Brian laughed and pointed out the window. It was a billboard of two Americans, one white, one black. In cartoon balloon-talk one was saying, "Baseball Brand is too muchi." The other replied, "Yeahbaby."

EIGHT

TAKE A MEETING

O n Monday I walked into the office laden with gifts and called out, "Ohaiyo gozaimasu. Good morning." Instead of the usual responses, there was dead silence. No one would answer me; everyone looked displeased with me. I asked Takagi-san what the problem was.

"It would be better if you spoke to Kamakura-san," he said, curtly.

I turned to Kamakura-san. "Is there something wrong?"

He stared at me with disdain. "You have committed a grave transgression. How could you have done such a thing?"

I was mystified. "What did I do?"

"Your vacation," he growled.

"What about it? You gave me permission to go."

"Did you ask the personnel office?"

"No," I said, bewildered. The thought hadn't occurred to me. Everyone had approved, no one had objected.

Kamakura-san looked stiffly at me. "The personnel office is furious at this snub. They have told me, your group leader, not to let you back to work until you obtain their permission. I have informed the team that you are not to be spoken to until the all-clear signal is given."

I nodded. "Right," I said. I parked my shopping bags full of obligatory gifts and headed downstairs.

Saito-san, in personnel, said, "How could you have let your team down by ignoring Sony's vacation policy?"

"You never explained any vacation policy."

Saito-san stiffened. "That's because you had no need to know it."

"I see."

"You're only a trainee. No one takes off four days in a row, certainly not a mere trainee. Your whole group is annoyed and disgusted by such behavior."

I saw that no explanation I could make was acceptable. There was nothing to do but make a formal apology, which I tendered in my very formal Japanese, the only form I knew. With my apology to the Personnel Department accepted, my redemption was complete, the slight mended. The "all clear" signal was passed to my group leader, and from my group leader to my teammates. I returned to my desk upstairs. Everyone spoke to me again and happily received their gifts.

●

The four of us Luce Foundation *gaijin* tried to keep in touch and to keep up one another's morale. It was terrific just to hear American English over a meal or on the telephone. So even as my hopes of learning the wonderful management techniques of Japan seemed to slip away, or we struggled with housing and various cultural differences, we kept each other going through our contact.

Joel and I especially kept up with each other's adventures. At our first dinner together in November, we commiserated and joked and the discussion came around to my reprimand and the question of individuality in Japan. No one at Sony had anything like my ego-bound individualism. Why?

I was reminded of our seeing a group of schoolchildren on their way home from elementary school our first afternoon in Tokyo. We had been surrounded at knee level by a sea of bright yellow raincoats: shorts, little hats, and backpacks all exactly alike. Since then, we had become acquainted with the more somber school uniforms of the older children: the girls navy blue middy blouses and skirts, the boys black or navy uniforms with brass buttons, respectively modeled on the seamen's uniforms of the German navy and on Prussian army uniforms, nations once admired by the Japanese for their disproportionately great power, achieved through discipline, subordination to the group, and technological prowess. It was with outmoded but effective German canons that the Japanese devastated numerically superior Russian forces in 1905, the first defeat ever of a modern Occidental power by an Asian nation. That it was due to imported technological superiority was not lost on the Japanese.

The educational approaches were as uniform as the youngsters' dress. Absolutely all students received the same instruction, regardless of whether they were of average intelligence, academically superior, or even learning disabled. Everyone was taught exactly the same material the same way at the same time. Individual needs were not recognized and did not receive specialized attention.

Classroom discipline consisted primarily of being ostracized. Kids were punished either by being ordered into the corner to stand silent, staring at the wall, or by being ignored by classmates, just as I had been at Sony. Even in adulthood, to be removed from the group was the most serious punishment for a Japanese.

The group was all. Without it you almost didn't exist. Personal allegiance was subservient to the group's interest. It sounded positive, selfless: workers labored for the good of the company and their fellow group members, enduring long hours and work weeks to achieve collective goals. Everyone took care of everyone else, even a foreign newcomer like me. On the downside, however, if you were suddenly not part of the group or put in Coventry for having put personal interests above the group's, then suddenly no one cared about you at all, until some time passed and you were reinstated just as suddenly or someone in authority restored your membership.

The pressure on students was tremendous. From preschool on, barring holidays, children attended school eleven months of the year, 240 days to an American kid's 180. Cram schools—*juku*—abounded and were patronized from the earliest ages, because even passing the tests for kindergarten was an academic milestone for which children crammed mercilessly in private tutoring schools. They studied to the near exclusion of all else. To get into the right kindergarten, which was connected to the best high school, and, in turn, to the finest university, was absolutely crucial and central to the child's (and the parents') existence. A student improved his chances of success significantly by getting onto the best track, and there were actual accounts in the daily newspapers of five- and six-year-old failures committing suicide under the unrelenting pressure.

I told Joel about my Japanese roommate in grad school. For all four years that he studied in the States for his doctorate, he never once went home. He had really wanted to a few times. But taking a break from his pursuit of the degree for any reason whatsoever was unthinkable. His family, especially his father, would have interpreted it as a shameful and total defeat if he went home empty-handed. When his brother was getting married, he was sent plane tickets but to no avail. He did not once go home, not for his brother's wedding, not even for his mother's funeral.

Joel and I had also been brought up, of course, with the idea that to be successful human beings we had to compete hard. But we were also urged to respect and develop ourselves as individuals in order to successfully interact with others and to lead full lives. Our idea of a group, a team, was a collection of competitive individuals who had won their places and now would each try to make his mark and reap whatever rewards were possible. This was totally contrary to the upbringing of everyone around us in Japan. Inherent in the Japanese concept of group was self-sacrifice for the greater good.

Here the well-being of the group was everything. A team was like a chorus, and certainly not a collection of stars. It was not everyone for himself, albeit jointly. One was even willing to take less of a piece of the pie and, in so doing, augment the share of others who otherwise might not have had an equal-size piece. One increased one's share of the pie by increasing the size of the pie. More people could work because wages were not the maximum one could command. By permitting financial room for more people to work, the economy as a whole benefited and grew, which of course increased everyone's individual share. By accepting less, the theory went, you ended up with more. That at least was the overt philosophy.

We talked about our fellow Scholars and we talked about our culture shock. "Speaking of which," Joel said, looking chagrined, "I find myself forgetting the English for some things."

"Me, too," I confessed.

"Really?"

"Yes, Joel-san. Just hang in there. It's exhausting to concentrate so hard on a foreign language. You start forgetting your own. My grammar and word order in English have also gotten a little strange, if that's what's getting to you."

Joel looked mildly relieved. "Would you mind telling me something then?"

"Sure."

"What," he said, "is the English word for 'the day that preceded yesterday'?"

It took me a minute to think about the question. Then I said, "Ah, Joel."

"Yes?"

"There is no one word in English for 'the day before yesterday.'"

He knitted his brow. "Do you think we've been here too long?"

•

Since I still had no real work to do in the office, and since Saito-san, in personnel, and Takagi-san, my immediate supervisor, had not come up with anything tangible, I scouted around for some on my own.

Rob Nelson, one of the few American employees in Sony's Tokyo headquarters, proposed that I help edit an instruction manual for the new personal computer Sony was about to release. It was called Hit Bit.

I leapt at the chance! It wasn't management but it beat sitting at my desk doing busywork. Over in Rob Nelson's division I was given a workstation, the Japanese instruction manual for the new PC, and the proposed English translation. A meeting would be held in a few days to discuss the strategy for marketing the machine in English-speaking countries, and various European and American staff were invited to attend, myself included.

Reviewing the manual and the plans, I concluded that the project was seriously flawed. It was fortunate that a major meeting had been called as there were many significant changes to recommend before this PC would stand a chance in the American and European markets. I gave Nelson my evaluation. He said, "You're right," and invited me out after work.

The evening's group consisted of some of our colleagues, Nelson, and myself. Our destination was Shinjuku, probably the largest entertainment district in all of Japan. Nelson, a true expatriate, was fluent in Japanese and promised to translate everything, besides showing me a good time.

Shinjuku's streets were narrow and teeming, offering pleasures of all varieties. There were restaurants, bars, movies, live shows, and sex of every conceivable variety. Just as our group left the shelter of the train station it started to rain. We headed into the back alleyways, cramped and cluttered even by Asian standards. One of the men suggested we stop somewhere for some *shochu*. I assumed he meant for us to take shelter in a warm, dry bar. Instead, he found us a tiny stall with walls made of discarded crates and a roof of plastic sheeting. The counter was a stack of rough, splintered boxes along which stood a motley assortment of students, unwashed vagrants, construction workers, and white-collar office staff, many of them carrying pocketbooks looped on their wrists in the fashion popular with Germans.

Nelson ordered us some *shochu,* at about fifty cents a shot, and I got a steaming hot glass of the raw potato liquor. I watched my fellow carousers and imitated the way they gingerly held their glasses so as to avoid scalding my fingers. I brought it to my lips slowly, hesitantly sipped a bit, and nearly choked. My eyes teared. I glanced around at the mob in the makeshift roadhouse. Everyone was jostling, elbow to elbow, consuming the firewater.

Across the way was a magazine stand selling magazines with flesh-filled covers. Ironically, Japanese pornographers protected the identities of female subjects by superimposing black rectangles over their eyes. Neither could pubic hair be shown, so the offending regions were airbrushed, blurred, or blacked out. Frontal nudity was unacceptable in magazines. Despite the official prudery, massage parlor ads often preceded otherwise innocuous films at public movie theaters, I had noticed, and one rather daring television channel was known around town as the Blue Channel. No rectangles or air brushing there. Even weekly news glossies had ribald cartoons and several color pinups of buxom blondes.

I asked Nelson about the various kinds of establishments along the alleyway. He said there were simple bars, hostess clubs where female employees flirted in a randy manner with male patrons who bought them overpriced drinks for the privilege of their company. The cabarets were about the same but also had topless waitresses or dancers and entertainers. He pointed out a massage parlor, a coffeehouse, a Turkish bath, and a love hotel. The first three, he said, would have prostitutes; the hotel might provide them or a guest could bring his own. *Mizu shobai* it was all called: "the water trade." All of it for men only.

When customers got tired of the voyeuristic and other pleasures marketed in places like Shinjuku, they might book a special tour to Bangkok or Manila or some other exotic port of call. The tours were very popular. We finished our scorching liquor and went once again out into the drizzle.

The next stop was a *pachinko* palace. The fluorescent lights were bright and the noise of the vertical pinball-like machines deafening. Everyone seemed to be shouting. The frenetic machines whirred and clicked as the metal balls inside them were released from one level down into another. Players were mesmerized; the tension in the room was palpable. You would have thought the jackpots were vast, but they were only trinkets: bars of soap, key rings, toothpick holders.

Then it was off to a club for some drinking. With Nelson translating, I was startled to hear the men openly venting their resentments about their workplace and even insulting their bosses. I couldn't believe what I was hearing: complaints, jibes, parodies. Nelson saw my surprise and explained. The basic idea was this. Everything could be expressed while drunk, or at least feigning intoxication. It was understood that the next morning, when everyone was sober, none of what was said would be remembered or repeated. Meanwhile, this cathartic charade allowed them to get things off their chests without doing themselves any damage professionally.

A waitress passed by wearing mostly her order pad.

"I'm glad I married a Japanese wife," Nelson said, surveying the revelers. "I haven't been home once this week before eleven o'clock."

Ikeda-san went over to the *karaoke* machine—a portable cassette-tape player with loudspeakers that played background accompaniments. A microphone with an echo-chamber effect allowed even the worst amateur singer to sound like Frank Sinatra when crooning the lyrics of a song through the amplifying system. It was like having a back-up band in the shower with you.

Ikeda-san let loose with an *enka*—sad songs about loves lost and times gone by. They were incredibly saccharine ballads. "Sweet, sweet, and sweeter," Nelson said.

It was clear from the horribly off-key renditions, heartfelt expressions, and occasional tears that *karaoke* was another acceptable means of publicly venting one's stronger emotions. I asked Nelson what *karaoke* meant. "Empty orchestra" was the rough translation.

As Ikeda-san belted out another tearjerker, tears came to my eyes. It wasn't that his interpretation was that moving, but the air was thick with cigarette smoke. Japanese men chain-smoked.

We ate and drank until it was time to catch trains for home. As we headed for the station, we joined hundreds of other inebriated *sararimen* staggering arm in arm to their trains. The more seriously drunk were being prodded into taxis by bar hostesses and dispatched home to their dutiful wives. On the platform, in the near distance, I could see men in suits urinating on the tracks, and someone nearby made a crack about golden arches. As I walked through the remains of people's dinners and various waste products around the station, I asked my colleagues about alcoholism and received their assurances that there wasn't any: "We Japanese have no problem with alcoholism."

●

A few days later the big meeting about Hit Bit was convened in one of the large conference rooms. I was introduced to seven executives. All of us wore our gray Sony vests, but our relative ranks were readily apparent. The senior manager had walked in first and sat down first, opposite the door, followed by the next highest-ranking manager, and so on down the line, until the pecking order reached me, Gary-san the trainee, and I finally entered and sat. The Americans present were invited to open the discussion, which seemed to me a cordial gesture.

Nelson, a full-fledged Sony employee, began. Although he was fluent in Japanese, the meeting would be conducted in English, in deference to the Westerners present. Nelson pointed out that the name Hit Bit was not a good one for the U.S. market. While it derived from the phrase *hito-bito,* "the people"—and thereby had some connotation, like Volkswagen, that it was a computer for the common man or the nation—in English it just sounded odd. Hitting a bit made no sense.

Also, the friendly puppy dog chosen to illustrate the user's manual, was inappropriate. It would not appeal to business executives in the United States, Rob said. Quite the contrary. The fifth-grade reading level and the language employed in the manual was so patronizing and simplistic that, in combination with the cute puppy, the machine would be mistakenly viewed as child-oriented. Worst of all perhaps, the manual was totally unorganized, the information just thrown together in whatever random order it accrued. There was no step-by-step logic. The operator would have to read all the directions through and try to figure them out for himself, if he could.

It was a pretty thorough indictment of the marketing strategy for Hit Bit and I anticipated that there would be strong reaction and a lot of discussion as the magnitude of the questions raised dawned on those in charge. In fact, there was no evident reaction, and no discussion. The meeting proceeded as if nothing critical had been voiced. In short order the marketing plan was approved, the meeting adjourned.

The Japanese executives had reached their decisions privately, before the meeting. They had felt out each other's opinions, doubtless in the nonassertive conversational style I had learned from my teammates, and arrived at a consensus. No real exchange was anticipated at the meeting to which Rob and I and two European employees had been summoned. It would have been bad form to allow discussion and disagreement here. In "front" (*omote*), in an official group gathering, there could only be unanimity. Disagreement or conflict was inappropriate and unacceptable within the group in this out-front setting. Differences between members of the group were settled in "back" (*ura*), and then only in oblique, nonassertive fashion. Our mistake was in thinking that the meeting we were summoned to was taking place in back (*ura*) amongst members of the group — ourselves. We now realized we had only been invited to the formal ritual of the *omote* meeting. We were not privy to the earlier informal session where the real decision making had gone on. We were not "in" (*uchi*), within the group, we were outside it (*soto*), and in dealing with us as outsiders the group members presented the standard united front that permitted no compromise or concession, and certainly not a rejection of the decisions already in place.

We Westerners had been kidding ourselves. What we were dealing with in Sony, and in all of Japan for that matter, were interlocking homogeneous groups the sum of which was one self-sustaining homogeneous racial entity that had existed for many centuries. For all their absorption in imitating American things, the Japanese remained an ultraconservative group, extraordinarily wary, and well defended against incursive forces that might threaten their homogeneity and purity.

The last to enter, I was the last to leave the ceremony. I gathered up my things and dejectedly returned to my desk in the Computer Division. Once again I met with a cold reception. This time I wasn't surprised. It did not matter that I had done the sensible thing in taking on the temporary assignment with Rob Nelson, since I had no other real work. It made no difference. In leaving, even temporarily, I had become an outsider; one could not belong to several groups simultaneously. I had abandoned the team and would be ostracized, I guessed, at least temporarily.

Decisions, like my undertaking the Hit Bit project, were not seen as selections. One did not select a particular soft drink; one sided with Coca-Cola, or Pepsi Cola. Being part of or siding with two groups simultaneously was not conceivable. I had sided with the International Division and was being made to pay a price as a kind of social restitution. Indeed, a few days later I was forgiven again and restored, but I did not care nearly as much this time around.

●

I wasn't happy in my work. I needed advice. Perhaps foolishly, I turned to Mr. Morton's aide at the Asia Foundation office. I thought Nakano-san might have witnessed similar situations and be able to advise me. It was a mistake. Although I had specifically asked him to keep my inquiry confidential, I suppose he assumed indirect communication with his superior, in oblique Japanese fashion, was my real intent. In keeping with this cultural norm of using go-betweens instead of confronting, Mr. Morton did not call me directly to talk about the situation. He spoke, instead, to the other three Luce Scholars, with the expectation that they would transmit his message to me and, of course, they obliged.

At Joel's urging, I telephoned Mr. Morton and he invited me to come down to his office for a chat. I wondered if he knew that I had tried to go around him by writing to the Asia Foundation's program director in San Francisco, describing my language problem and my frustration at the endless mandatory lectures and meetings, all in a language I could not hope to understand with less than three or four years of full-time language study.

Ushering me into a chair, Mr. Morton said, "I've received a copy of your letter to San Francisco." The directness caught me off guard. "You really shouldn't worry about these things. I spoke to Sony yesterday and was assured your Japanese is improving. You no longer have a language problem."

"Ah—"

"As for wasting your time in meetings, you will learn, as you get older, that everyone feels frustrated by the time wasted in meetings. It's inevitable: a price one must pay."

"Mr. Morton," I said, "no matter what Sony says, my Japanese is years away from everyday business use. The meetings I complain about attending are held in Japanese I don't understand."

Mr. Morton looked miffed. "Didn't we just agree?" he said, with a faint tinge of impatience. "Sony thinks your Japanese is fine."

I sighed. I wasn't getting through to him.

"Now," he said, "what I'm not happy about are your dorm problems." Just then the telephone interrupted. "Excuse me," he said, as the phone continued to ring. "I must step out for a few moments."

He was gone for some minutes. I glanced around his comfortable office and my eye fell on some letters, neatly spread out on the coffee table. By odd coincidence, they were letters about me, letters of reference I had supplied with my application to the program. The letters were personal evaluations of me, enumerating positive and negative aspects of Gary-san. The more critical passages, I noted, were daintily underlined in red.

Mr. Morton returned. By then I had had an opportunity to get his message. Namely, others had criticized me in the past, therefore I was not always right. I was, in fact, wrong now: My criticisms could be easily rationalized, as he had demonstrated. I should be more humble, more docile, and stop making difficulties.

There was no confrontation, no direct discussion even; Mr. Morton had been in Japan a long time. But the message was conveyed—indirectly, as was appropriate, given the setting.

Returning to my regular desk across town in the Computer Division, I was glum.

"Gary-san," Maruyama-san said, "don't look so sad."

"I would really like to know how to communicate in this country," I said, sounding frustrated.

"Listen to me, please. We are all trying to help you, but in a Japanese way. It may seem slow, and even wrong, to you, but you will be better off if you just view our way as different."

"I guess I'll just have to try harder," I said.

"Perhaps not," she said. "Maybe that is the American way. We Japanese don't see trying harder as the only solution. We say 'Shikata ga nai,' which means 'It can't be helped; there is nothing we can do.'"

"Shikata ga nai."

"Yes. We must accept things beyond our control."

I nodded; I got the picture. If there was nothing anyone could do, no one could be singled out as blameworthy or responsible. Rules were rules, orders were orders, no matter how rigid or arbitrary, or even counterproductive. In accepting things as they were, the need to look any further for a solution to a problem was eliminated and the frustration at being powerless to effectuate change was glossed over, buried. Hopefully forgotten. The Japanese I had encountered seemed content with their lot, true. But they did not seem happy. The problems of crowding, sexism, and a rigid conservatism seemed obvious, as did the surprisingly low standard of living compared to the United States. Yet as I often heard Japanese tell one another, what they had was good enough. After all, they were only an island country.

As if to exemplify what she was advising, Maruyama-san announced that she was being sent to learn the APL computer language. I asked why. She looked bemused. She had no idea; it hadn't even occurred to her to ask. Sony, she assumed, had a project that required knowledge of APL. What it might be was not her concern. I nodded. *Shikata ga nai.*

Nohara-san looked less resigned to his news, however. There was some supportive clucking around him that sounded a bit like commiseration. My attention turned to him. It had been rumored earlier that morning that he was again being reassigned abroad.

He had spent four years in Great Britain and the United States and had been back in Japan only a few months: just long enough to settle in, renew old friendships, reacclimate himself. Now word had come that he was going back to the States once more, this time for two to three years.

For the briefest moment he seemed dismayed. Recovering quickly, he said he would sell the house he had just bought and search madly for a wife. Thirty-three and still a bachelor, he was well past prime marital eligibility. But even if he were to find a proper wife in the time remaining, taking her with him would be difficult. Then, if they were to have a family soon, it was likely she and the child would return to Japan, for there were serious social dangers to children remaining abroad too long, primarily having to do with their socialization and education.

Someone Westernized was not acceptable back in Japanese society. If, while overseas, children picked up foreign attitudes or received a Western education, they faced a rude awakening upon their return in that they would no longer be considered fully Japanese. And in a system where one's education was so literally one's future, they might actually be denied admission to Japanese schools and find themselves outsiders in their own country, as extreme as that might sound. Japanese were part of the national group so long as they remained the same: in their education, upbringing, and social attitudes. Anyone raised or educated outside that system was suspect.

My own two Japanese friends, who had been in graduate school with me in Los Angeles, had initially been intimidated by the personal freedoms they had in the States. Over time they became accustomed to greater personal freedom and choice as evidenced by their more relaxed and self-assertive behavior. Returning home to Tokyo, they found that unless they relinquished their Western ways they would not be accepted. Meeting them on Japanese soil, they seemed to me to have undergone a profound readjustment.

In the afternoon we took our exercise at our desks and at the tea break cajoled Nohara-san, hoping to buoy his spirits.

NINE

ARRESTING DEVELOPMENTS

J t was mid-winter. The Tokyo heating season was well under way. In the office we wore short-sleeved shirts and sweltered, in the dorm the situation was not as consistent.

The company dormitory was centrally heated, unlike private homes, which relied on costly electric space heaters or employed *kotatsu*, tables with heating elements underneath and, often, draped with material that preserved the warmth when you sat with legs tucked under it. At night most people slept with blankets and the heat was cut off.

At the dormitory the heat went on each weekday at 5:00 P.M. and went off promptly at 10:00 P.M. In the early evening the building was unbearably hot. After ten it was advisable to get into your futon before the room became too cold. Falling asleep was comfortable; waking up, in a room so cold that you could see your breath, was not.

I asked Hashimoto-san if there was any way I could control the excessive evening heat in my room.

"No, you can't do that," he said.

Instead of fighting the system, I adapted, Japanese-style. I opened my windows wide and balanced the oppressive heat with the chill wintry air.

As if to compensate for the overheating during the week, on weekends Hashimoto-san provided no heat at all. Most of the dorm residents cleared out and went home, but I had no nearby family to flee to. I asked Hashimoto-san if perhaps on weekends I might avail myself of a tiny space heater, as it was so very cold both day and night.

"No," said Hashimoto-san. "No."

No matter what day of the week, every morning when I entered the men's bathroom, Mrs. Hashimoto would be there, doing her wash before the open windows and exclaiming, "Samui! Samui!" Meaning: "It's cold! It's cold!"

On the coldest winter morning I entered the bathroom, teeth chattering, and suggested to her that it might be less cold if she were to, just this once, close the window.

"We can't do that," she admonished, and continued complaining about the cold: "Samui! Samui!"

"Shikata ga nai," I said: It can't be helped.

Mrs. Hashimoto beamed. "Hai!" she exclaimed, happy that I was finally getting it.

"Que sera sera."

"Hai!" she said, looking puzzled.

●

Whenever I spoke to any of the other Luce Scholars it seemed that we were forever complaining to one another about persistent minor ailments. No one ever seemed well. We all had lingering colds and aches and seemed to be suffering some kind of malaise that eluded definition. We figured we had some kind of Asian bugs to which we had no acquired immunity.

In addition to my running inventory of chronic ills, I added a sore shoulder, a souvenir of a pickup basketball game back in California. I had suffered a shoulder separation and in the chill Tokyo winter, the shoulder hurt.

It was suggested I visit the company clinic. There, a series of physical tests was recommended, as well as a psychological exam. I was mildly surprised at the latter but intrigued by the prospect of seeing a Japanese psychological test.

The psychological test came first and consisted of Rorschach ink-blot interpretations and a fill-in-the-blank test, both administered in Japanese. The results, I was assured, would remain confidential. The physical examination took place in the Sony infirmary where a highly-respected staff physician questioned me in halting English, probed, poked, and quickly ascertained my problem.

"You have a serious shoulder condition," he said, "but there is no need to worry." Then, without further explanation, he produced a hypodermic and instantly administered an injection. "I will arrange everything," he said. "I am acquainted with the best hand surgeon in Japan. He will operate on you this Saturday."

Hand surgeon? Shoulder? Operate!

The prospect of undergoing surgery in a foreign country at the hands of a surgeon with a speciality unrelated to my problem, and for a condition that was more uncomfortable than dangerous, left me dismayed. When I related all this to my teammates, they nodded gravely. Takagi-san suggested that doctors knew best. Everyone concurred.

They seemed surprised that I should be thinking twice about

it and were relieved to hear that I hadn't questioned the doctor about his diagnosis and recommendation of immediate surgery. That would have been unbelievably rude.

The doctor was a *sensei* like my Japanese-language tutor, but even more of an authority figure. Much greater. To challenge his judgment, to even contemplate a second opinion, was unthinkable. Absolute trust was a necessary bond in any doctor-patient relationship.

The company doctor sent a message that he had set up an appointment at a local hospital for the following morning for further examination. I felt relieved—and reprieved—and appeared promptly the next day at 9:30.

The hospital was not what I had anticipated. It looked as if it had been built during the Second World War under austerity conditions. There was a loud clamoring mob in the lobby and it took me some time to find someone who spoke English. I asked why all these people were there. The administrator said, "Take a number." I surmised the rest.

Soon there was a line that snaked out the door. My number, I was informed, would not be called upstairs in the clinic for several hours. This was how medical appointments worked: You made a date for a time that was within two or three hours of your turn, and you waited. I went out and walked around for ninety minutes and came back. They were nowhere near my number, and I decided to look over the clinic facilities.

The stairs to the fourth floor sounded as if they were about to collapse. Upstairs, the halls were drab and dimly lit, nothing like the sleek, modern facility I had first expected. There was nothing high tech about it. In the clinic portion the benches were filled with patients and family members. Someone in white approached me and asked as to my business there. I told her, whereupon she instructed me to drop my number card in the box and wait there for it to be reached. I complied and sat down. In just ten minutes my name was called.

"How could you have reached me already?" I asked at the desk.

"Well . . ." The nurse hesitated, shifting uneasily. "You are an American," she said, "so we cannot have you wait."

I was made uncomfortable by this preferential treatment but not so uncomfortable that I refused it. An attendant showed me into some kind of combination ward, laboratory, and clinic, all jammed together in one room. It was crammed with desks, staff, equipment, and occupied beds. A half dozen doctors, surrounded by interns and residents, were treating patients in this cramped area. Out of the jumble emerged a doctor, who greeted me. He heard my medical history and did some tests, then referred me to yet another doctor who would see me the next day. With my chart in hand, I withdrew and went home.

Doctor Number Three was in private practice and, I assumed, would be very punctual. As luck would have it, I awoke late and rushed like mad to his office. Like banks and public clocks, Tokyo's subways always met their posted timetables. I ran for the train, even remembered to run up the left side of the stairs, thereby avoiding the usual disastrous results of charging up on the right, and I flew into the car at the last possible moment.

Arriving at my appointment, I staggered in, breathless and unfed but precisely on time.

"Chotto matte kudasai," the receptionist said, meaning: "Please wait a moment."

I found a seat in the crowded waiting area and scanned the periodicals. They were mostly *manga,* and men's magazines full of sports stories and scantily clad women. After half an hour I asked if perhaps I had missed hearing my name.

"Chotto matte kudasai," she said, very softly and sweetly. After forty-five minutes, I meekly asked again, and inquired once more after an hour had passed. The earlier reply was repeated each time. The wait seemed so odd in a country that prided itself on such punctuality in the workplace, in public transportation, school. Other than the previous day's wait, this was the longest I had ever waited for anything since arriving in Japan. Finally I realized it was a code: The receptionist was simply employing a polite expression to inform me that I would have to wait as long as I would have to wait.

Taking in the situation, it was clear that five or six patients were scheduled simultaneously. This was in stark contrast to the scheduled efficiency of the society at large, which, by now, I anticipated. Suddenly there would be these pockets of mad imprecision and ambiguity. However, a patient would never complain to a doctor who had kept him waiting, and I was not supposed to complain either, about anything, ever.

The doctor prescribed several medications and the prescriptions were filled right there. In Japan, doctors served as physicians and pharmacists both. From a vast wall of little drawers, off in a supply room that resembled a herbalist's, came my medicines, each wrapped in blank paper, with no label on the outside or on the bottles, envelopes and little boxes inside. Just as with the inoculation, I had no idea what these medicines were that I was supposed to be taking. In fact, I was amazed patients didn't regularly dose themselves incorrectly, given the absence of instructions or identifying labels. But this was the normal practice. In fact, instead of being hesitant about this, my fellow patients that day were adamant that they should be given pills, liquids, powders, or whatever else the doctor might part with. It seemed to be an article of faith that medications should be given.

Finally examined, I trudged back to the office, feeling the onset of yet another cold. Takagi-san and the others urged me to take my pills and powders but I was reluctant. They thought nothing of it: One never asked a doctor what it was they prescribed. When no one was looking, I abandoned the stuff in my desk drawer.

My cold was getting worse but I was determined to go the course without any more time off until the Christmas/New Year vacation, when I hoped to head south with Joel. I sat at my desk, feeling miserable, sneezing, sniffling, and blowing my nose, until I started noticing the looks directed toward me.

Maruyama-san came over to my desk after lunch bearing a pack of tissues, some cough drops, and my favorite candies. Her show of concern lifted my spirits. Unthinkingly, I reached out to her affectionately. She recoiled and pulled away, turning dark red with embarrassment. Physical contact and shows of emotion were totally unacceptable. I had seen the most innocent contact produce profuse apologies and embarrassment. Before I could say anything, a loud sneeze seized me and she escaped.

Kamakura-san took me aside.

"Don't you know sneezing is rude?"

"No," I said, somewhat surprised. All I knew was that a good *sarariman* never took sick days just because he had a cold. What was I supposed to do?

"Well," he said, exasperated, "if you must sneeze, please be polite about it and don't blow your nose afterward."

●

*O*n Saturday, instead of having surgery, I went to Disneyland. It was unseasonably mild and seemed reasonable,
and I had heard that everything at the theme park was American
and in English: "an American experience." Besides, I needed to
think about things.

Seated on the train out, I watched a group of *sararimen,* sitting
opposite, each well attired in plaid sports slacks, peaked cap,
and insulated windbreaker and carrying a full set of golf clubs,
on their return from a morning on the links. Green fees, I knew,
were unbelievably high in Japan, something on the order of
$100, but the game was unimaginably popular. During week-
day lunch hours, on hundreds of Tokyo rooftops, men with
determined expressions patronized driving ranges to practice.
Golfers worked at the game with steely concentration and near
total dedication. It was their *re sha,* a transmogrified form of the
English for "leisure." The Japanese meaning was closer to
something like "a programmed nonworking activity." It was
another borrowed pastime that the Japanese pursued with near
abandon.

As the train came to a stop, the four golfers rose to say good-
bye to one another. To my surprise, instead of bowing they
partook of a ritual I had not seen Japanese perform before: They
shook hands. I guess it went with the game.

Disneyland was, as advertised, a complete transplant, and
wildly popular. It would have been odd to spend a day in Tokyo
without somewhere glimpsing a Disneyland souvenir; the Disney characters epitomized the cloying cuteness, called *kawaii,* so
endearing to the Japanese. It was a bicultural fit.

Great effort, I could see, had been devoted to making the
park entirely and authentically American. The food was all of
the hot dog and french fries variety; no *obento* box lunches were
even permitted inside. The signs were almost entirely in En-

glish and English was the working language, although few of
the signs or announcements could have been comprehensible to
the Japanese.

On Main Street stood Mickey Mouse and his friends surrounded by Japanese kids and adults. Like the golfers on the
train, Mickey and his pals shook everyone's hand.

●

Bingo! Personnel came through. I was being reassigned and
I was happy.

I sailed into work, changed into my vest, and took my place
in the Computer Division where teammates were exchanging
greetings and bows. I wished Takagi-san a good morning. He
said, "Today you will begin a project in International Marketing. After the eight-thirty buzzer, please report to Yamada-san,
the general manager of the International Marketing Division.
His desk is on the fifth floor."

At precisely 8:30 the buzzer sounded and Takagi-san reminded me that it was time for me to leave. I took the elevator to
five and got off. All the signs were in Japanese; I was lost. A
passerby stopped to direct me, but I couldn't understand a word
he said. I showed another man the slip of paper with Yamada-
san's name. He said something. Seeing my incomprehension,
he motioned for me to follow him and led me to International
Marketing.

The office looked very much like the Computer Division: a
large room ringing with the noise of telephones, voices, office
machines; a sea of desks and bowed heads. Electric fans scat-
tered here and there ineffectively stirred the oppressively humid
air, while outside December winds howled. The only immediate difference was the total absence of women.

"Welcome to International Marketing," said Yamada-san in Japanese, accompanied by a deep bow.

"Pleased to meet you," I replied, with a slightly lower, longer bow, so as to show proper respect.

"Takagi-san ni yoru to anata no kyomi wa computaa da soo desu."

I hadn't understood a word. In my best formal Japanese, I said, "Excuse me, but I don't speak Japanese very well."

"Oh," he said, in heavily accented English, "I see. I said that Takagi-san informed me you have an M.S. in computer science and an M.B.A., and that you are eager to study how Sony does business."

I beamed. "Yes. I have read so much about Japanese management that has impressed me greatly. I have come to Japan to see it in action."

"Good." He nodded. "We have some exciting things to teach you. Here, please have a look at these."

He handed me several papers. All were written in *kanji*.

"I am sorry," I said, in my stilted Japanese. "I have only studied a few months and do not read Japanese writing well."

"Is that so?" A brief silence ensued between us, even in the hubbub that surrounded us. He began again: "One of our current projects is to uncover reasons for different sales patterns of our Walkman in the United States, Europe, and Japan. We would like your help."

It sounded great! Yamada-san described the department in considerable detail. As he spoke, the phone on his desk rang. It was for me.

"Hello, Gary-san." It was the assistant manager of the Computer Division, Kamakura-san. "Are you in the International Marketing Division? The location card on your desk says that you have gone home for the day. We were worried."

I had not set the cards, thinking they knew where I was. "I am sorry," I said. "I forgot to set my cards. Could you please set the correct one for me?"

"I will do it, this time. But do not forget again."

I thanked him and hung up, and Yamada-san continued.

"Before you start on this project, we would like you to come to our team meeting so we can all get to know you and find out all your interests. The meeting will begin in twenty minutes, more or less," he said.

"Yes," I said. "May I wait in your office until then?"

"Office?" Yamada-san said. "This desk is my office."

●

I sat in the meeting room with twelve other men positioned around a long table. The ventilation was even poorer than in the main room. It was stifling.

Yamada-san introduced me in English as a trainee on a scholarship from the United States. "Now let's talk about the Walkman market analysis project," he said, and switched to rapid Japanese. Everyone began to scribble notes in his little white Sony notebooks. I sat, straining to catch whatever information I could. I understood nothing of substance. Someone turned to me and asked something in Japanese. I said my Japanese wasn't good and that I didn't understand what he was asking, but the man didn't understand my English, so Yamada-san had to translate. What he had wanted to know was what might interest me in relation to the project.

"Perhaps I could do the pricing study," I said. "Different prices for Walkman would have their effect on market share."

Yamada-san said they would consider that. Or, I suggested, I could look at advertising costs in each country. They would consider that seriously as well. The discussion resumed in Japanese; my attention wandered. "What do you think?" Yamada-san said, startling me.

"Could you be a little more specific?"

"We have decided that, since you are technically trained, you should do a statistical trend analysis of sales over a period of time. In this way you will get a true understanding of Japanese management." He smiled. "We are glad you will be working with us."

The meeting ended. I was given over to Ikeda-san for further briefing. He said, "I . . . to you . . . explain." It was all downhill from there. Finally, I interrupted, saying that I could not follow his explanation. He looked hurt. Yamada-san was summoned. He explained.

"We would like you to find out the patterns that have occurred over the last few years with Walkman sales. Mr. Ikeda will furnish you with data."

Hooray! I was excited. It was the kind of unstructured problem that appealed to me. Yamada-san continued:

"The project will involve organizing the data by continent and then by country. We want to look at sales by season, item, and by price, over time."

"I can suggest several other good ways of analyzing such data," I said.

"Yes," he said. "We have much data. We need someone to plot the points. Ikeda-san will tell you what graphs to generate. Your job will be to connect the sales points. Perhaps, as a computer expert, you will write a program to do this. This will be interesting and informative for you."

I looked at the data. The task was simplicity itself. "After I plot the points, what analysis should I undertake first?"

"Analysis?" he said. "You are a trainee. You plot the points. Ikeda-san will do the analysis."

Day after day I plotted points. As soon as I finished one graph, Ikeda-san produced another nearly indistinguishable set of data.

I plotted points like a kid connecting dots and delivered the graphs to Ikeda-san and never saw the graphs again. Ten days of plodding point plotting. On the eleventh morning Yamada-san came by to thank me for all my labors.

"We are all very happy with your work, Gary-san. We are pleased to give you such a good opportunity to learn about Sony. When this project ends, we may ask you to stay on. We would like you to plot points for the advertising study we are doing. In that way you will also learn all about advertising strategies."

Perhaps somewhere in what I had worked on there was some intellectual challenge, but it had not been evident to me. Politely, in my textbook Japanese, I declined.

●

Back once again in the Computer Division, I tried proposing my own project.

I had studied Management Information Systems (MIS) in business school. Sony's Computer Division was having trouble with theirs. One manager showed me the book on MIS he was reading to try to catch up on advanced information. For all its mighty strides in computer hardware, Japan was two to five years behind the United States in software development techniques. It was a surprising lag, given the reputation for efficiency and planning, but it was most definitely there. Software was always the most expensive part of any computer-based system. Consequently, huge sums were expended for its development and maintenance, and the less advanced the software, the less efficient the computers. Sony's managers had neither the time nor the expertise to do such a survey and evaluation, and it would be extremely useful to the company.

The several people I approached seemed to like my idea. I pressed forward, excited and encouraged. But nothing came of it.

"We've never done anything like that before" was what I kept hearing, after the initial receptivity.

Nohara-san, his departure for the United States growing closer, took me to lunch and did his best to console and explain.

"It is the 'we' that is significant. The managers have pride. They would feel deflated if an American could do something they couldn't, especially one who is only a trainee."

I gave a dismissive shrug.

Nohara-san continued anyway: "Naturally, they will be reluctant to try something that hasn't been done before. They fear failure and the loss of face that would come with failure. No matter how you phrase it, Gary-san, the managers in the division will never accept your help with this MIS survey."

He was no doubt right. He was raised in Japan and had worked in the United States. He probably understood both cultures the best of anyone I worked with. Still, it was discouraging. I would never get anywhere staying where I was in Sony, so I took another crack at the personnel people.

After lunch I went once again to Saito-san and made yet another pitch for a job change — Legal, Research, anywhere they employed English a lot. His usual response to my entreaties was that they would be seriously considered. This time he said it would be strongly considered. I took him at his word and returned to my desk.

Nohara-san and Maruyama-san knew what I had been up to. They sat me down in the programming area and I sensed something serious was coming.

"You are misinterpreting the message you are being given about other work," he said. "They are just being polite."

"Yes," Maruyama-san agreed. "It is *tatemae*."

Nohara-san nodded. "*Tatemae* is to 'stand in front.'"

"A facade," I said.

"Yes, yes. Just as *hai* does not really mean 'yes,' but merely is an acknowledgment that you have been heard. When they say that they will do their best or consider your requests, these are only polite ways of saying 'no,' Gary-san. You understand."

"Yes," I said. "I do. You find it in America, too. It's called 'the run around.'"

TEN

A NIGHT AT THE OPERA

oel came up with some opera tickets. Not Japanese opera, grand opera: *The Bartered Bride* by Smetana. At the theater, while we waited for the curtain, Joel related his most recent Mrs. Nishiyama adventure. He had met a young woman from Toyo University and, although they weren't remotely serious, they had started going out; it was an interesting friendship for each of them. Mrs. Nishiyama had mistaken Toyo University for Tokyo University, the top school in the country. So she was pleased by their association. When she discovered her error, all hell broke loose.

Mrs. Nishiyama hectored Joel about this "degrading acquaintance," spoke to the young woman scornfully whenever she called, failed to convey phone messages to Joel, and once even hung up on her. Joel was to be protected, at all costs, from this inferior person from a slightly lower social class.

Joel was upset but he had to admit that it was funny, too, and we both laughed. At least he had a social life about which Mrs. Nishiyama could be alarmed. Mine was extinct.

The theater was jammed, a full house, and the curtain went

up. The Bohemian atmosphere was meticulously re-created on stage and the Czech peasant costumes were lavish, but it was an adjustment to hear the opera performed by Japanese in Japanese.

We were to meet Taro Nishiyama afterward and left promptly at the final curtain to rendezvous. Taro drove up and stopped at the curb, then was peremptory about the need for the two of them to go right back to the Nishiyama household. His mother had fixed dinner, he said, for the whole family, and was awaiting them.

Joel sighed and looked exasperated. "I specifically said I'd be home late and wouldn't be having dinner."

"Maybe she thinks you're out on a date," I teased.

Joel gave me a look. "I'd better go," he said. "A few nights ago I said I'd be home by half past eight and didn't finish at the hospital on time. By quarter to nine she was deeply distressed, and at nine she called the police. I'd really better," he said and got in the car.

It sped off. I sought out one of the myriad street vendors, who materialized every evening in Tokyo, and contemplated female psychology as I slurped noodles alongside a half dozen other bachelors.

●

Maruyama-san was about to have a birthday, Takagi-san mentioned one morning, and impulsively I decided to defy the fraternization ban. Takagi-san and Nohara-san had effectively chaperoned our occasional dinners after work and enough was enough. I asked her out—just the two of us.

She accepted.

Somewhat taken aback, I said, "Ah, where would you like to go for dinner?"

"You must choose," she replied.

I suggested an Indian restaurant in the Roppongi district and Maruyama-san agreed to meet me there after work as we could not possibly be seen leaving Sony together.

"By the way," I said, "how old will you be?"

"Saaaa." She dallied, then changed the subject.

"You know," I said, "I don't think I've ever asked you what sort of work your father does."

"Oh," she said, "he works. You know."

The restaurant was on the seventh floor of an office building, a not uncommon location in space-scarce Tokyo. Many sat atop skyscrapers, especially in Shinjuku. When the menus were presented, I blithely selected something for myself. Maruyama-san pondered. She was still scrutinizing five minutes later and finally asked me to order for her.

Talking to her alone was fun but I noticed she hardly touched her food. After dinner, I took her for tea and French pastry and asked her how the restaurant compared to others she had been to. "Others?" she said. She had never been to another Indian restaurant in her life, she confessed, and said she had found the food "interesting." I knew what that meant.

When I pressed her as to why she had not expressed a preference for some other sort of cuisine, she just said that I had been nice enough to treat her; the implication was it wouldn't have been polite. She looked at her wristwatch.

"Do you really have to go so soon?"

"Oh, yes. My parents are waiting up for me."

She stood up and I got up, too. She smiled sweetly, thanked me very much for taking her out, apologized again about her long commute home, and vanished.

I sat back down. Maruyama-san was the best woman friend I had in Japan. We had spent hours in the office talking. Yet, after all this time, I still knew nothing at all about her. She asked questions sometimes, but she did not answer any.

The evening was still young and I decided to cheer myself. I splurged on a taxi and headed off to Kabukicho, the entertainment district. The strip was ablaze with neon and smoldering desire. Clusters of men strolled through the district, bar hopping and gawking. Zoot-suited barkers gently tempted them to try the pleasures of their establishments. I went into a hostess bar and waved off the several offers of company, preferring to drink alone. When my second beer arrived, I noticed a really striking young woman on the adjoining barstool. She looked as if she came with the cover charge, but there was something about her that seemed unrelated to the gaudy saloon. She could certainly pass for a bar girl, dressed as she was in a halter and hot pants, but she wasn't being terribly ambitious about it if that was her job. I caught her glancing at me—a sensation not unfamiliar to *gaijin*—and I used it to start a conversation.

She was refreshingly relaxed and candid. I had guessed wrong: She wasn't a hostess. She actually worked across the street in a massage parlor and was taking a break. I tried the Japanese equivalent of "What's a nice girl like you doing in a place like this?" She laughed and said, "Making money. Lots of it."

In her off hours she was a college student attending one of the two-year schools where women commonly matriculated. She was, she said, accumulating as much cash as possible so she could buy a house and use it as an equity investment because she knew her career after college would be short-lived. By twenty-seven it would be all over and she wanted the security of the property to offset the inevitable loss of income after her employer stopped giving her raises and promotions as he edged her out. The only means and the only time available for making such money was now and at the massage parlor. I asked her how much a massage cost and how much of it she got. The price was 10,000 yen; she got half. She was, she said, a good negotiator.

By day, a college coed; at night, a prostitute. I knew I should be disapproving and critical, but instead I found myself admiring her forthright spirit. How many other college girls were in her line of work? Quite a few, she said, surprising me once again.

She had to go, break over. I was trying to be cordial and simultaneously to calculate the exchange rate on 10,000 yen into U.S. greenbacks: $40.

"Well, good night," she said and left, framed for a moment in the doorway against the ephemeral flashes in the street.

I breathed deeply and said, "Sayonara," knowing I would hate myself in the morning.

●

Bored, I decided to broaden my social horizons. Somewhere I would meet an English-speaking Japanese girl. I tried CommInn, a coffeehouse with the express purpose of bringing together those wishing to speak English. In fact, only English was permitted on the premises and at a handful of other similar coffeehouses in the city. Practicing English was a near national obsession.

CommInn (an embarrassing play on "Come in" and communication) was a tiny single room, again in an office building, on the fifth floor (really the fourth). The furnishings were bare and basic, like the two owners stationed at the front desk, greeting regulars. The patrons were Japanese and Westerners and the place, I soon discovered, was usually filled with a bizarre mix of bilingual Occidental and Japanese gentlemen,

Japanese ladies, and American sailors from Yokosuka. Despite the English-only rule, most of the Japanese spoke little English, so many of the conversations in the room consisted of the usual ritual: "Where are you from?" "Do you teach English?" "What do you like most about Japan?" Even worse, many of the women were wary of "advances" from foreign men.

Ironically enough, some of the most conservative personalities I encountered were hardcore expatriates. Many seemed to have not only picked up the language and mannerisms but had also adopted, with off-putting zeal, incredibly critical postures concerning Europe and especially the United States. They had become Japanophiles and, to some degree, renounced and denounced their first cultures, almost corroborating at times the exaggerated notions of the Japanese about the depravity and violence of Western society. It was odd to listen to and stranger still to converse with them on these subjects as we sat overlooking the lights of the nearest entertainment district.

I did meet Dr. Yoshi, a medical resident who spoke English well and had wide interests in music and literature. We struck up a friendship and had dinner together several times at some of Tokyo's more interesting restaurants. He was unusual, an urbane man with a questioning approach to the world that was surprising.

Then a most unexpected thing happened. I went to hear a talk at the English-language school and was looking around when I heard a lovely female voice explain the various programs being offered. The listeners were polite Japanese men; the speaker an attractive Japanese woman. I struck up a conversation with her. She kindly answered me in simple Japanese, enunciating slowly. This was her part-time work, she said. She was a student. As we chatted on, conversing became increasingly difficult and she and I had trouble understanding one another.

I finally said, in Japanese, "Could I try to talk to you in English?"

"Whew," she said, "that would be a relief. My name is Margaret Chow, I'm Hong Kong Chinese, here as an exchange student. And I'm having a devil of a time learning Japanese."

I would have supposed our experiences in Japan would have been very different. In fact, we had much in common. As Margaret put it, "On first meeting, the Japanese treat me well—like anyone else. But if they guess or if I mention that I'm Chinese, then they treat me like a *gaijin*."

She held forth on the treatment of Koreans born in Japan, how Korean restaurants were disguised not to appear Korean, how Koreans were discriminated against in housing and jobs, how there were few Korean goods in Tokyo, a city where you could buy absolutely anything—except maybe an argument or a Korean export. No public violence, no shouting matches.

What, she wanted to know, was my opinion of their glossed over histories of conflicts with Korea and China and other Asian nations they had tried to dominate by force of arms. I said I wasn't aware of how history was taught in Japan. She gave a short laugh. "Smoothly," she said, "with many 'unfortunate conflicts' and 'military advances' that elsewhere were commemorated as massacres."

We discussed the *burakumin* as well: the descendants of butchers and tanners stigmatized by their ancestors' involvement with something this Buddhist society considered profane: namely, the carcasses of animals. Because their predecessors had performed work as butchers and tanners and the like, they now were relegated to menial labor such as street cleaning, discriminated against in their housing, and stuck at the foot of the socioeconomic ladder for the duration of their lives. Even worse, they passed this on to succeeding generations. In Japan, where everyone's business and life is everyone else's concern, and one's every movement is recorded at some level, all family geneologies were readily available and accessible and always checked whenever references were required. So there was no escape for the *burakumin*. The social fabric was so tightly drawn, and every strand so well documented, that no one could pass themselves off as anything else, or change their name and thereby elude their fateful membership in this underclass.

I had even heard there were registries cataloging *burakumin* that companies checked before accepting applicants for any position. She said that the Japanese usually denied their existence or, at the very least, minimized the situation if they could not avoid the topic entirely. In a similar vein, Japan did not readily accept refugees from other Asian countries or offer assistance to underdeveloped nations. When pressed, the rebuttal was often, "We are only an island country."

She asked if I knew the translation of the word *burakumin*. I said I thought it meant something like "village people." She nodded. And did I know the meaning of the word when written in Chinese characters? I didn't. "Excessive filth," she said.

●

The office was a bore. I was reduced to "reading" memoranda, in Japanese, that were routed to me and everyone else on the team as a matter of course. I would initial the memos, even though I could not understand the contents, and

pass them along. When I protested the silliness of this procedure, I was asked to continue initialing anyway, as "it would
look better."

I also occasionally read correspondence and memos written
in English and helped translate these. And that was about it.

My *senpai*, Takagi-san, knew how bored I was, but he was
having his own problems with the firm. The head of the division, Murata-bucho, had given him a significant project to
work on at long last, and Takagi-san had plunged in. He was
determined to show what he could do. The project was a
comprehensive evaluation of various computer languages and
the recommendation of the best of them for use by Sony. He had
done terrific work. Murata-bucho read his report, praised him
for his effort, and then completely disregarded the study. It
might as well not have been prepared.

Takagi-san tried to remain equable, but I could see that he
had been crushed anew. I would catch him staring and looking
somber. Was he seeing himself years hence, a *sarariman* and Sony
middle manager for whom there was no room up ahead? Was he
seeing himself occupying one of the *mado giwa* or "window
seats" to which excess talent was relegated, sent to the periphery
where he would remain for the rest of his career, side-tracked
and stuck, unable to move up, and unable to get out of Sony and
into another job with another company. Meanwhile, lacking
promotion, he might be given tedious tasks, assigned to distant
company outposts far from Japan and his family, and maybe
even forced to accept pay cuts or demotion. Promotion was not
always a panacea either. The surplus of middle managers was
also forcing the creation of higher titles without real jobs. There
were a lot of those around, too. Takagi-san insisted nothing was
the matter, but I could sense the despondency in the utter

smoothness of his composure. Too much equilibrium. At times he came in hungover. Occasionally he would be late.

The fact was that Japanese management techniques, such a craze in U.S. business schools and in the American press, did not really work as they were alleged to. Japanese companies, including Sony, neither operated according to an egalitarian bottom-up decision-making corporate model, nor evinced any interest in communication directed from the bottom upward. Instead of the hyperbole and elaborate organization charts of Japanese management that I had been treated to in school at the height of the Japanese-case-studies craze, the actual nature of corporate organization and functioning bore a curious resemblance to Japanese feudal society.

The lower member, the *kohai,* learned by watching his *senpai,* the senior of the pair. The *kohai* would watch and assist and ask questions. Seniority determined superiority.

I could only communicate with my *senpai,* who would relay my information to the *kacho,* who would speak to Murata-bucho, who was equivalent to a feudal "lord," and so on up the line. If, at any level, anyone senior and superior elected not to convey the communication, it simply died there, and this was the normal course of the rare request or suggestion that might be launched upward.

At the top of the company, any Japanese company, were those who had attended the most prestigious universities. Those so privileged formed the pool from which employers chose the top people in the firm. The pool also constituted an "old boy" network within and across companies, and within and across government ministries. They were a predestined elite, and there was precious little they would ever listen to from down below.

The celebrated and much written about workers quality circles were marginally successful, but on the most elementary level. Anywhere above the production line the weekly meetings were ceremonial window dressing, the formal rituals of Japanese groups. My co-workers, especially the younger ones, were clearly bored and privately contemptuous of the time-wasting pretense of airing problems and proposing things to higher management. Decisions came from the top. The bottom-up nonsense was the stuff of American editors' dreams and theorists' rhapsodies: utter nonsense that we had perpetrated upon ourselves and perpetuated in our media-driven culture.

But how, I wondered, given the rigid hierarchy, the wasting of effort and spirit, the time conceded to ceremonial group harmonics . . . how, with all that unnecessary baggage, had Sony been able to create and develop its many innovative products for which it was now so famous. In roundabout fashion I posed the question to a younger colleague. He sniffed, disdainfully, jealously. The answer was simple. Designers in the New Products Division did not have to play by the same rules. They were exempt. "Understand?" The rest of the company was just the delivery system.

"Yes," I said. "But what is all this uniformity and harmony about then, if the real heart and engine are separate from it."

"Imeji," he said, and I laughed. *Imeji*, taken from the English "image."

Uncertain whether I understood, he said, "Tatemae. Yes?" I nodded. "Yes, 'facade.'"

●

It was December and Christmas in a Buddhist country. The 109 department store in Shibuya was adorned by a huge Joseph and Mary. They were, however, in modern clothes and could have been mistaken for Bonnie and Clyde in their natty outfits, except for the halos ringing their heads. It was not a religious holy day or a holiday, but after work all the shops, boutiques, and major stores all over Tokyo were bursting with people partaking of the year's traditionally biggest shopping spree. And everywhere I went I could hear Beethoven's Ninth Symphony played over the public-address system. There were, in fact, classes offered all over town where you could go to learn to sing "Ode to Joy" from the Ninth's last movement, inexplicably so.

Mr. Nishiyama invited the four Luce Scholars to his company's Christmas and New Year's party. He introduced us to the managers and we watched the celebrants play a game that consisted of naming the zip codes of various towns. Afterward we were invited back to the house for another dinner. There was something creepy about the way we had been passed along at the party and stared at, so we were happy to get out of there.

Entering the living room, we were greeted by Mrs. Nishiyama, who once again complimented me on my Japanese. We chatted briefly until dinner was announced in the living room. Mrs. Nishiyama brought out a huge tray of food—seaweed, rice, and the ingredients for sushi rolls that we made ourselves. As soon as anyone finished, she piled on more. As we ate, Mr. Nishiyama took photographs.

After dessert we returned to the living room. There were the clarinets, waiting, and the same librettos. Taro and Joel played woodwind duets, the same exact selections we had played last time. Mrs. Nishiyama beamed. Mr. Nishiyama photographed us and, this time, tape-recorded our performance. I was prevailed upon to play my original compositions on the piano and, not having composed anything new, I played the same pieces once again. The camera flashed intermittently, I squinted and smiled and played on. The festivities ended and we took our leave. A few days later I received another set of photos to commemorate the occasion.

As the New Year approached, the country shut down for a national holiday. Joel and I headed for Kyushu, the southernmost of the four main islands that constitute Japan, and Ann decided to come along for a few days. We took the overnight train south. It was packed. There were only three major annual holidays during which the Japanese can travel and this was one of them. All of us were worn out and looking forward to some warm weather and each other's company. Mrs. Nishiyama wisely had reserved sleeping berths for us.

I always carried little *kanji* flashcards on trains, local or long distance, and I studied them when there was sufficient room to move my arms on a commuter train or subway, so I was well practiced and had little difficulty in working with them aboard the sleeper. As usual, the cards brought forth mouth-covered giggles from schoolgirls. I guess they found it absurdly amusing to see an adult who couldn't do what they could. I didn't mind the giggles at all, but it was particularly frustrating that the many hours spent studying seemed to produce so little progress. I could study for hours on end, week after week, and show little improvement, then suddenly move up to some new plateau of mastery and realize something really difficult now appeared simple. But then I would remain plateaued at that new level until once again the same odd process occurred and my skills would surge forward and stop.

In addition to the schoolchildren peering in at the *gaijin,* as bedtime neared a procession of older Japanese men paraded past in their underwear, brushing their teeth. Then it was lights out.

We had just gotten off the train the next day, when Ann realized she had left her travel bag aboard. "Oh, God!" she gasped. I told her to calm down and we went to inform the stationmaster. Ann was resigned to the loss: her camera, money, passport, registration card. The stationmaster, however, urged her not to worry. Completely confident, he contacted the train. Her handbag was found immediately, still at her seat, untouched. Two stations up the line it was taken off and delivered intact to Ann a few hours later. This was, after all, Japan. Or so the stationmaster seemed to imply, although modestly.

Disaster averted, we continued on to Miyajima Island, famous for wild monkeys and a temple that appeared to float when the tide was in. We came upon a crowd in a small town and stopped to see what the commotion was about. At the center of the gathering were four men and a hollowed out tree stump. In the stump was some dough. The men began to pound it with long mallets while the crowd around them chanted. Farther back, women sang traditional songs accompanied by the banjolike *shamisen*. A whisper went through the crowd; evidently *gaijin* were uncommon here. One of the men stopped pounding. He looked me over, then handed me the mallet. Another gave Joel his, and we joined in the celebration, pounding the dough for the first rice cakes of the year. There was an openness and friendliness that I had rarely experienced in Tokyo.

Ann returned to Tokyo, but Joel and I continued on to southern Kyushu where we had been invited for New Year's by the family of a girl named Saori, whom Joel had met through Taro. The train was packed like a sardine can, standing room only. It was so crowded the conductors didn't even try to collect tickets. We arrived to find the family preparing for the big holiday that would begin that evening.

New Year's Eve started quietly enough with visits from family friends and the appearance of family albums and accompanying stories. As midnight approached, everyone huddled around the television set to watch the annual special featuring the latest pop singers and performers, and that was pretty much it. In the morning Saori and others started things with a traditional trek up the neighboring mountain to watch the sun rise. I passed on this opportunity, but accompanied the family to their first—and probably only—visit to a shrine that year.

Saori looked ethereal in her elegant kimono. I expressed regret that women did not don these remarkable costumes more often. "No, no," she protested. "They are crushing. This kimono is so tight, I can hardly breathe. They are very uncomfortable."

The shrine was cut into the side of the mountain, and it was mobbed. Celebrants washed their hands in the river and in stone cisterns before offering prayers, others were buying special arrows and souvenirs or trying various delicacies, and still others were hanging little slips of paper on tree branches. Joel and I also bought some of these slips containing our fortunes and wrapped them onto the branches so they could come true. The trees on the grounds were white with fluttering bits of paper.

You prayed by ringing a special bell to wake up the *kami* or "gods" who lived in the mountain. Then you clapped three times and made your New Year's wish. Amidst the carnival atmosphere, some Japanese were actually praying. Among them, inside the shrine, was a man praying earnestly. But instead of holding a traditional offering of fruit or flowers, he held in his hands a golf club.

Saori saw my puzzlement and explained: "On New Year's Day people pray for those things most important to them. In earlier times it was health, happiness, security. In modern Japan, however, people pray for better test scores, new cars, or, like that man, a lower golf handicap."

Joel and I thanked our hosts and pushed on. We ferried across the bay to Kagoshima, where we wandered through another shrine celebration and bumped into three Westerners in their twenties. The three young men were Mormon missionaries, going door-to-door in the hope of finding receptive hearts. Their mission was for six months; they had been at it for three. The Japanese, they said, were extremely difficult to reach, much less convert. One asked if we wanted to hear about Joseph Smith. I declined.

We reached the southern resort town of Ibusuki, across the bay from Sakurajima, an active, real-live volcano, throwing up lava and rocks in the distance, whose geothermal action made the beach sand warm and steamy.

Toward evening, Joel and I went into a bathhouse, undressed, and put on thin cotton robes. With nothing else on except turbaned towels, we ran out into a shocking blast of cold air. Our teeth chattering, we scrambled down the steaming beach through the waning light until we came to a large canopy. There were dim lights beneath it but apparently no people. A glance downward, however, revealed rows of heads wrapped in white towels sticking out of the sand like cabbages in a garden.

From out of the dusk materialized three sprightly grand-mothers with shovels. They were the "gravediggers," they teased, and promptly set to work excavating our plots. The ladies excavated two steamy holes and had us lie in them. They worked expertly and we were quickly planted in the furrows of turbaned heads peeping out of the sand. Clearly amused by the novelty of *gaijin* visitors, the grandmothers struck up a conver-sation with their two captives, their chatter full of sexual innu-endo, especially when we wriggled from time to time in the volcanic heat. The air was probably forty degrees; the sand, eighty-five. After a while the warmth was like a narcotic and I nearly drifted off to sleep. I was brought back only by the sounds of Hawaiian music wafting down from speakers in the canopy above. I wasn't dreaming; for some reason the lush twangy melodies were part of the experience. In the distance loomed the volcano's rim.

After our sandbaths Joel and I looked for other amusements, but the town being what it was—a hot-spring resort—everything involved bathing of some kind. Before the Meiji Restoration, bathing in public baths and hot springs was mixed, with men and women unabashedly sharing the same facilities. In traditional Japanese thinking, there was nothing shameful about the unclad human figure. With Western contact came barriers. Baths were segregated. Now only amongst the older generation, and in rural areas, could you still find mixed bathing.

We asked the youth hostel manager for directions to a public bath. He told us of several nearby but advised against one in particular. Joel asked why. "Saaa . . ." he said, sucking in air, "it's a little . . ." He stopped again, obviously embarrassed, then finally confessed that it had mixed bathing. We thanked him for his help and headed right off to the place he had warned against.

"Jungle Bath," Joel said, reading aloud the sign over the door to what looked like a huge airplane hangar. It was enormous, steamy, and full of palm trees. There were fifteen different natural thermal pools in a variety of sizes, shapes, temperatures, and even mineral contents. Customers varied as well, coming in all sizes, sexes, and ages. Each bathing pool also differed in motif: oasis, tropical isle, jungle grotto. The Japanese liked themes. Bathing was mixed throughout, except for one pool reserved exclusively for women of a more Western modesty, but even that had been invaded by Japanese males who stared openly at the naked women.

Joel and I were determined to try it out, cultural inhibitions not withstanding. When in Rome, or Ibusuki. In we went, sans togas, and it was very enjoyable, although the place did seem like some kind of concrete manifestation of the puzzling and contrary Japanese and Western cultures co-existing in Japan.

In the morning we went on to Beppu, a hot-springs town on the northeast coast of Kyushu. Immediately adjacent to the train station was the red-light district, its myriad neon lights flashing above the great variety of pleasures offered beneath them. These ran the gamut from bars, hostess clubs, teahouses, cabarets, massage parlors, Turkish baths, love hotels, and "No Pants" *kissaten* (bottomless teahouses). Technically, prostitution and brothels were illegal, and had been since the Occupation, when American custodians had imported their own native American ideas of morality. In fact, prostitution was common. Sexual services were even advertised in fairly respectable weeklies, the advertisements done in catalog style, accompanied by pictures and descriptions of those offering their services. One upscale scheme in Tokyo, known as the "Love Bank," had an illustrious clientele of prominent businessmen, professionals, and politicians. In return for substantial membership fees and dues, the "club" offered the men mistresses. It was extremely popular and profitable; several young women made their fortunes. However, when the arrangements were publicized, the scandal ruined a good number of careers and the "Love Bank" went under.

We strolled through, feeling jaded. There wasn't anything here we hadn't seen elsewhere in Japan; such areas, after all, were nearly as common as railroad stations. But then we came upon something quite unusual in the guidebook. "But how are we

A NIGHT AT THE OPERA

going to ask anyone for directions to this?" I said. Joel came up
with the idea of asking for the exhibition with the "special
theme." The first few people we stopped just looked at us funny,
but an old lady in her seventies somehow got the hint and,
giggling, sent us off into the back alleys. We searched around
and found nothing but what looked like the gates to a shrine. I
was about to suggest we give up, when my companion pointed
out the admissions booth just beyond the archway. We paid up,
500 yen, and went inside.

"What do you think?" Joel said.

I shrugged. "Never saw anything like it."

It was, we were confident, one of the planet's few phallic
museums. Showcased were all kinds of specimens, imaginable
and unimaginable, as well as an assortment of erotic art, most of
it cheap and tawdry, some of it ancient and exquisite. There
were also a few mechanized dioramas, depicting such Walt
Disney innocents as Snow White and the Seven Dwarfs, all of
whom came disturbingly to life at the push of a button. "Hi
ho," I said, yawning.

We passed up the souvenir stand and set out for the train back
to Tokyo.

ELEVEN

ROOM AT THE TOP

A stack of mail awaited me at the dorm, including a letter from Brian and Pat's friend, Margo, thanking me for my generous offer to squire her around and show her the sights. What offer, I thought. Oh, well. There were also some lovely New Year's cards, many of them from my co-workers. There was one from Nakamura-san that was, I thought, particularly kind. It actually extended an invitation for me to come to her home after vacation.

The next morning I thanked her for her kindness and thoughtful invitation.

"Oh, that," she said. "My mother thought it would sound nice to write that to a *gaijin*. It isn't really an invitation, you understand."

"Oh," I said, "I see," and retreated.

Later, one of my teammates stopped by my desk and casually told me that the results of my psychological tests were in. He escorted me to the infirmary because the psychologist, who had interpreted the results, spoke no English. So much for confidentiality, I thought.

The psychologist, a pure Freudian, had derived her conclusions solely from the test results; she and I had never spoken directly and I wondered what she might have made of my responses to the Rorschach blots, especially given the linguistic and cultural barriers. Without a moment's hesitation, the doctor set forth her diagnosis and my teammate translated. I had severe developmental problems. I was mired in some particular stage that I could not make out.

"Please," I said, "could you repeat that?"

My translator obliged: I was, it seemed, stuck at the "prenasal stage."

"Prenasal?" I said.

"Yes," he said, oddly pleased.

Furthermore, the doctor had concluded, since my mental health was precarious and my problems so deep-rooted, I was unfit to work at Sony. For the good of all, she was requesting that I be returned to the States for further treatment of my prenasal condition.

I thought it all mildly amusing until she announced that these confidential results had already been sent to my manager and the Personnel Department, along with her recommendations. My translator teammate blithely added that my team members had also been informed.

Upset now, I asked how she could have done this without my knowledge or consent, especially as the test was understood to be confidential. She seemed mildly surprised. She had maintained confidentiality, she insisted; the results had remained within my group.

When I returned to work, my colleagues gazed at me somberly, with pitiful expressions one might give the sick or wounded. Mental illness was the utmost disgrace in Japan, as I knew, so now I was really in for it. How could I have been so stupid as to playfully take their test out of curiosity.

Ashamed for me, no one said a word. Later, personnel offered to arrange treatment by one of the top psychologists in Japan, a short two-hour commute from the city.

Mr. Morton called soon thereafter from the Asia Foundation. When I got to his office, he was unusually direct, telling me that Sony had informed him that I was psychologically unsuited. I pointed out the circumstances of the test and told him the psychiatrist's diagnosis. To his credit, he actually laughed out loud. I sagged in my chair, relieved.

Fairly confident that Mr. Morton would pull some of his many strings within Sony, I returned to work, such as it was.

•

The weather turned cold. Temperatures dropped to sub-freezing levels and a snowstorm buffeted the city. Streets were glazed with ice. The steep slope I had to negotiate on my way to the office was suddenly an ice slide. I slid, then slipped and fell—hard—onto my back, the wind knocked out of me.

It was 8:12 A.M. on a main street in Tokyo, with everyone rushing headlong to their workplaces. Except me. I lay there writhing, airless, and in pain. Not only did passersby not stop to help, they walked right over me. No one lent a hand. Directions or gallant gestures to visitors were one thing, but I was clearly a stranger, not a tourist but an outsider, and a problem in my literally fallen state. So I was tuned out and passed by, and actually stepped over as if I weren't there.

I recovered my breath, if not my dignity, and trudged to the office. At work I was informed I would be given a project in February and that I was to spend the interim four weeks preparing for it by reading manuals. Although I suspected I was once again merely being put off, I decided to try it the Japanese way, not squeak my wheels, not stick out. I said thank you and took the manuals back to my desk.

●

Nohara-san's reassignment was imminent. He was a real friend and leaving yet again for a long stint abroad that he did not want. He had sold his recently bought house but he had not managed to find a wife, and one would be hard to find at the age at which he would return. At his going away party he gave his farewell speech in English and I translated it into Japanese for the group. Brideless, he left Japan a few days later with not a word of complaint.

After Nohara-san was gone, Kamakura-san "reassigned" me to a new lunch group—his own—and what had been the highpoint of my workday became as flat and tedious as the computer manuals I was reading. Had I come all this way to read a computer manual or to find out everything I could about Japanese management? I glanced around the humid, stale room, jammed wall to wall with books, printouts, computer terminals, people. What was the truth about this? All those heady lectures, books, and articles about their corporate culture and management techniques. Akio Morita, businessman, entrepreneur, an egalitarian employer, owner of a gray vest like the rest of us, his door always open. A man who had studied American culture up close, knew it better in some ways than the natives, to whom he sold them brilliantly designed electronic goods based on their own unused patents and virtually discarded technology. He understood Americans; he spoke perfect English. He would know what I was talking about. What the heck. I made a lousy nail.

Summoning up some courage, I got up from my desk and straightened my papers. Where was I going, someone asked. To see the boss.

Floor Six. The rest of Sony was well marked but the hallway here was bare. No signs. I found a blank door. I might have been mistakenly entering a janitor's closet; on the other side was an anonymous passageway. Way down that dimly lit hall I came to a set of swinging doors, and pushed through onto plush carpeting. A woman was seated behind a desk, Morita-san's secretary, I presumed. She was impeccably polite and gave me an appointment two weeks hence. It couldn't get any more bottom-up than this, I thought. I thanked her and left the same Alice-in-Wonderland way that I had come.

Back at my desk, I waited for signs of trouble. Nothing. Nothing happened and I went back to my manuals.

The two weeks passed uneventfully: obligatory morning farewell to Hashimoto-san, setting my dorm marker to *out,* breakfast at the commissary, at my desk by the 8:30 buzzer, manuals, lunch, exercise, tea break, manuals, Japanese practice, bath, bed.

My appointment was coming up. What would I say to this living legend? I tried not to think about it, it would just make me nervous. Then, on the Sunday before my meeting with him, Joel called me at the dormitory.

"I hear you're not going to work tomorrow," he said.

"Why?"

"I got a call from Mr. Morton yesterday. He said you had been terminated at Sony."

"Not to my knowledge."

"Yeah," Joel said. "Ken got a call about you on Friday. Morton phoned him, too. Said he hadn't been able to reach you."

"Gee, everybody's heard except me."

No one had told me anything so I decided to go to work anyway. They might be roundabout, oblique, indirect, and hammered down, but I wasn't. I was a squeaky wheel from the U.S.A. On Monday, in the middle of my Japanese lesson, the phone tolled. It was Mr. Morton.

"I am calling to inform you that you have been terminated by Sony and are to leave their premises as soon as possible. Sony hopes you will leave by this afternoon. But first, you must come down and see me. Right away." He hung up.

I was kind of shocked and elated at the same time. When I arrived at the Foundation offices, he was visibly annoyed. He said, "Sony claims they have to let you go because there was no way they could have met your needs, despite Sony's and my best efforts. I'm quite disappointed with your failure."

He paused. I said nothing.

"Will you be able to clear out this afternoon?"

"That's impossible," I said. "I can't pack that quickly and, even if I could, I have nowhere to go and no way to get there."

"Okay." He nodded. "I'll talk to Sony and try to get you a few days. But remember, you're no longer a Sony employee, so they no longer have any obligations toward you. If they want to throw you out, they can." He made some calls and arranged one more day.

That night I packed. Tuesday it snowed, and snowed. A rare Tokyo blizzard. I went into Sony and asked personnel for an extension on the use of my living quarters. They refused. Snow or no snow, shelter or no shelter, and regardless of any transport problems, I was to be gone by 5:30.

Hardball. By mid-afternoon the city was all but paralyzed: more than ten inches had descended, the worst storm in ages. I trudged to the Computer Division and tried again. No reprieve. Even my co-workers were surprised. Takagi-san called upper management and got someone high up to try. No deal. I kept squeaking. Finally Mr. Morton arranged for me to have until Friday.

Exhausted, I went back to the dorm, took a final bucket shower, and slipped into the scalding water of the bath. It still hurt. I settled down and tried not to disturb the steaming water so it would hurt less.

I reflected. The Japanese did not like complaints; I had complained. They liked indirection; I had been direct. They insisted on blind obedience and subordination to the group; I had intruded and protruded. I was a craggy black rock in their smoothly raked white pebble garden.

It was also pretty evident that unless you were born Japanese, you would always be outside. Membership was exclusionary, a privilege of race. Even those foreigners who had lived in Japan for a long time, or had actually been born here and knew the language, customs, and history better than some of the Japanese, were still not regarded as natives or fellow citizens. I had been accommodated as a matter of form, but there had been little of substance there. I padded back to my six-by-twelve room and stretched out on the futon, my head against one wall, my feet against the other.

The next morning I went to say good-bye. First Saito-san in personnel, the first person I had met my first day.

"It is too bad your experience had to end this way." He paused. "By the way, I wanted to tell you why you were pulled from the Research Division even before you arrived at Sony, and why you had never been transferred to any of the International Departments as you requested. There were secrets and sensitive proprietary material in those areas, and as a computer scientist, an outsider, and an American, you could not be trusted. Look at the IBM-Hitachi incident. One small leak to you—who could then sell the information to our competitors—and we would be in trouble."

Gary-san, industrial spy. I had sensed something like that and was happy to know it hadn't been paranoia. Well, at least it was logical, sequential, and candid, for which I thanked him.

I went over to the Computer Division and began saying good-bye. Maruyama-san said, "What has happened makes us very sad, but I, like many in the department, was shocked and disgusted with your behavior with Morita-san. We were all taken aback by your lack of respect in seeking an appointment with him. After all, not even the most trusted workers in Sony are allowed to ignore the proper levels of management and go right to the top. Such behavior shows flagrant contempt for seniority. If longtime employees cannot do so, it was particularly presumptuous of you, a trainee, to try such a thing. At that point, Sony had no other recourse. Your behavior could not be tolerated."

"Well, thank you for the explanation," I said. "I would like to keep in touch."

She hesitated, then said, "Hai."

Another female worker presented me with a Sony notebook, a parting gift, and asked me a question that refused to translate in my brain. It just hung there. What she wanted to know was: When would I prefer to have my farewell party?

TWELVE

JUST FRIENDS

J awoke Saturday morning, in International House, a free man. The sun was glistening on the clean white snow of the meticulously sculpted garden outside my room, and for the first time in a long time I felt at ease.

Mr. Morton was looking into a position for me at Tsukuba University. It was part of Tsukuba Science City, a large academic and research center sponsored by the government, a kind of Brasilia of the brainy that would concentrate Japan's best scientific minds on the development and application of new technologies. The scientists hated it because it was far out in the sticks north of Tokyo (although the city was rapidly growing out toward it).

The idea of being away from the districts I knew and my few friends did not appeal to me either, and I began my own job search, calling on old Japanese friends and acquaintances from graduate school. It was a good thing I did, too, because I sensed Mr. Morton was promoting my cause with less than terrific enthusiasm. As his assistant confided one day:

"Mr. Morton is quite displeased with you. He feels you have disgraced him in the eyes of both the foreign and Japanese communities."

I hadn't realized I'd caused such an international incident and said, "Why?"

"Your appointment was a personal favor to him by a friend at Sony. Since both Mr. Morton and his friend are highly visible in respected circles, your appointment, and now your dismissal, are public knowledge. Mr. Morton is embarrassed because he has lost face. All things considered, Mr. Morton possibly prefers to have you leave Japan as soon as possible."

Sorry about that, I thought. I had a couple of prospects: one with IBM Japan, the other with a small software house called SPEC. I would interview, and I would have some fun for a change.

Despite a terrible introductory gaffe (I had no business card to present upon first meeting) and despite my tortured, semi-grammatical attempts to expound on my credentials and business philosophy, SPEC liked me and offered me a position. Typically, however, they would not specify what I would be doing, and there was no polite way to ask. To most Japanese this lack of information wouldn't have made a difference. The only decision was whether to commit to the company and its will. Asked what he did for a living, a *sarariman* would not name the type of work but would simply name his company. Still, I hesitated to plunge, Japanese-style, into a job situation. The president insisted that he was fluent in English but would never speak any, and the other staff did not have any English skills to speak of. I decided to sleep on it and investigate my lead with IBM Japan.

Things went smoothly at the interview, conducted entirely in English, except for a question interjected by one of the men toward the end: "So why did you get fired from Sony?" one of the men blurted out. Despite this, IBM seemed happy with the prospect of having me. I decided not to worry while I waited for their final decision and concentrated on domestic life instead.

International House was comfortable and, more importantly, warm. There was central heating to be grateful for, and peaceful breakfasts overlooking a serene snow-covered garden. Also, it was near Roppongi, the high-class entertainment district that attracted a lot of foreigners. There were movies, expensive restaurants, classy bars, and teeming streets. The names said it all: The Almond Coffee Shop, Spago, Tony Roma's, and Fox's Bagels. Fox's had been set up by a transplanted American, presumably to serve the nearby foreign community, yet the shop had attracted Japanese as well. What was bagels and lox, after all, but smoked sashimi on bread. It tickled me to eavesdrop on the hunched, kimono-clad octogenarian matrons rave about the onion bagels and I became a regular patron. After a leisurely morning, I would stroll back to my room, greeting the neighborhood patrolman in his sentry box and chatting with him. Typical of these policemen, he knew every resident for blocks around and noted every irregularity and incident, however slight. Nothing happened on his beat without his knowing it. It was as if his nervous system extended out into the community and he could practically sense anything or anyone out of place.

In the evenings I spent time at CommInn, where I renewed my friendship with Dr. Yoshi and chatted with Saburo, the editor of an English-language magazine. Saburo invited me to a party and I went, expecting that he would have other English-speaking guests. However, I seemed to be the only one. The tiny studio was filled to bursting with guests, all speaking Japanese.

When I asked him if there might be somebody I could talk to, he took me off to a corner of his spartan flat and introduced me to a lithe young woman: "Gary-san, this is Hayashi Setsuko-san. Hayashi-san, this is Gary-san."

Setsuko's English was excellent, and she was intelligent and unusually direct. In fact, when she wasn't being disarming, I thought she was a bit arrogant. After an hour of monopolizing her, I asked her for her card.

"My card?" she said, with an almost angry intonation. "I am only an Office Lady. Why would you want to call an OL?"

But she produced one and I took it, wondering if I would. Actually, I thought not.

•

At the local convenience store I ran into Saito-san. He told me Sony personnel had received a call from IBM Japan. Trouble. Sure enough, when I called IBM about their opening, they said, "Unfortunately you may not be able to work for us after all." Which was Japanese for "No way!" It was sobering to think that if I had been a *sarariman* instead of a *gaijin,* this would have actually meant that I'd have been blacklisted for life. One phone call and your existence would be inexorably and permanently affected. I realized most Japanese pictured the United States as a kind of dangerous yet colorful frontier, a giant Dodge City, but I went off to the CommInn whistling "America, the Beautiful."

Dr. Yoshi invited me out: "I'd like to show you the beauty of the Japanese arts. May I take you to the theater?"

We attended performances of Kabuki and No. They were ancient forms: the atonal music, the use of masks and stylized gestures. We even watched some of the season's sumo tournaments on television. He asked me my impressions. In truth, I had trouble with it all, and told him so. After saying how much I appreciated his kindness, I confessed that I had been bored:

"I just don't get the point. Kabuki seems to me like so many costumed men singing like cats. The sumo matches look like a bunch of fat men throwing salt and grunting at each other."

He smiled. "That is because you are focusing on literal actions only. These performances attain meaning through symbolism. To appreciate them, you must know Japanese history and understand our concepts of trust, obligation, respect, loyalty, shame. Otherwise, yes, it can all be quite dull, excruciatingly slow and boring, even for Japanese."

It was true; I could most easily see it the next time I watched sumo wrestling. The tradition behind it, the styles and techniques, the rituals of the weigh-in and the blessing of the ring with the throwing of salt before each match.

I made an effort to understand and began reading about Kabuki and sumo and inadvertently came upon all sorts of fascinating symbolisms. Like the number four. Because it was pronounced the same way as the word for "death," it was considered terribly unlucky. Therefore buildings did not have fourth floors, and sets of anything—teacups, pens, golf balls— did not come in fours. On the other hand, all odd numbers were considered good luck, so sets came in odd numbers, pagodas always had an odd number of floors, and one holiday celebrated the children who were three, five, and seven. It was so strange. The irregular, the asymmetrical, the odd number, were all highly valued in this country so dedicated to conformity and uniformity and evenness.

●

J got another lead on a job and went around to be interviewed. The firm was Computer Services Corporation, otherwise known as CSK, Japan's largest independent software house. The president's assistant, Takahashi-san, interviewed me personally, along with four of his associates. Takahashi-san had a technical degree and a master's in business from MIT. Right up front I made sure he understood the insurmountable language problem I had experienced at Sony. He assured me my lack of fluency would not be an obstacle at CSK as I would be able to work in English, and he specified two very intriguing projects as examples. One was the development of a major research institute devoted to artificial intelligence. The other was to devise a strategy for marketing an artificial intelligence product that had been leased from a Silicon Valley company. At long last, I thought, and tentatively accepted the job right there.

Happily, I told my Japanese friends the news and got a flat response. They were surprised that I had "taken a step down." No one was impressed. In the past, when I told someone I worked at Sony it had elicited *oohs* and *ahs* and looks of awe. They respected me for my affiliation with a prestigious company. Since CSK was relatively unknown, and not among the top ten, they were less than enthusiastic.

I needed a new apartment to go with the new job and saw several miserable places: small, dark, run-down, high priced. The last flat I was shown was also decrepit and on the edge of Kabukicho, the home district of the Yakuza, Japan's mafia. The tiny first-floor apartment was in reality a single room. It had no running hot water or toilet and you had to bathe in a Japanese-style mini tub in the miniscule kitchen. I could see why the most popularly employed description of housing in Tokyo was "rabbit hutches."

Through a newspaper ad I eventually found a decent place, an "apartment" in a "*gaijin* mansion" not far from the Sony dorm. It was hardly a mansion but it was tall and fancy and that was enough to qualify. The *gaijin* appelation meant it had Western-style toilets and was occupied largely by foreigners. My new home consisted of a foyer and a single room that were engineering marvels. Every bit of space was functional. The front door opened just far enough so that it wouldn't block the kitchen portion of the foyer, on the left side of which was the closet and the ostensible galley kitchen, consisting of a tiny refrigerator under the sink, a single burner (no oven, of course), a counter board that fit across the sink, and a dish drying rack that fit over that.

Facing this arrangement was the "bathroom unit." It was a sort of plastic prefabricated room that permitted a single solution to the problem of installing Western plumbing in apartments that originally hadn't had them. The unit contained a tub, a sink with a hose that formed a shower, and the ultimate in luxury: a Western toilet. All these were made from the same plastic as the walls and ceiling, so the impression was that it had all been made in a plastic injection mold. That was the good news. The bad news was space. There was so little of it that a normal step out of the tub would put you in the toilet bowl, for instance. As for the rest, there was a bed with drawers underneath, a television, and, because it was a luxury apartment, a combination heater/air conditioner poised over the head of the bed.

It was unfortunate that they were both in the same unit and high up. The elevation was fine for the air conditioner part, but a heater on the ceiling was fairly useless. To remedy this, the unit had cleverly designed vents to direct the hot air down to where it would be most useful before it inevitably rose. Unfortunately, the vents didn't really work, so the room in winter was a gradually increasing continuum of temperatures, beginning with subartic around the ankles and building up to subtropical around the nose. This was while standing; when sleeping or lying down, the prone body was all at one temperature. However, the heat directed downward by the vents was so angled that one ear would be roasting while the other was freezing.

The balcony also had some drawbacks. It seemed like a nice place for dining al fresco but the heater/air conditioner occupied most of it. I didn't care. It was home. Through the sliding door, leading to the balcony, was the cityscape: buildings, flashing neon signs, and traffic congestion a few yards away. Best of all, it offered the rarest of luxuries in Japan, something for which there was no word in Japanese: privacy.

●

M argo. I had forgotten all about Brian and Pat's friend who was coming over, but as I wasn't due to start work immediately, I could show her the sights. I had met her for half an hour years earlier but barely remembered her, and then there she was, curly-haired, a mischievous glint in her eye, her five-foot three-inch form dwarfed by her enormous backpack. A traveler, I surmised.

Since there was hardly enough room for my shadow in my *gaijin* mansion abode, I found a decent *ryokan* for her to stay at. Still, her surprise on opening the door to her tiny and bare room was self-evident. "But it's empty," she said.

"It only looks that way," I assured her. "In the West nothing is nothing. In the East it isn't. What you are really looking at is a substantial nothingness — *ma*. For the Japanese, space has a kind of real weight, as a solid object would."

"What 'nothing' can I sit down on?"

"The Japanese," I said, "are a situational people. This room's use would depend upon the situation, the need. This tatami mat might serve as a couch. Roll out a futon and it becomes a bedroom."

"If you say so," Margo said, and dropped her backpack. "Whew," she said and began to unpack. All sorts of familiar items appeared from her bags. Vitamins (incredibly hard to find in Japan and expensive), big California oranges ($1.50 per in Tokyo), a huge box of Oreo cookies ($5 locally), and a box of Lipton's chicken soup packets (priceless). "For you," she beamed. "Pat and Brian said these were hard to come by in the mysterious East."

Margo was adventurous; she wanted to try everything, including every kind of lodging. After a few days at the inn, she wanted to try something new and I booked her into a "capsule hotel." These were budget-size accommodations, to say the least, compartments really. Each was about the size of a bed, more like cabinets set in a wall than rooms. You couldn't stand up straight in one of these as there was really only enough space to perhaps sit up and watch the television on the wall. Margo hopped in cheerfully, delighted by the exoticism, and invited me in, too. I scrunched up and visited for a while as we strategized a journey together.

We decided on Tohoku, the northeastern part of the main island of Honshu. It was said to be not only beautiful but also unfrequented by foreign tourists. It seemed to be the Japan of thirty or forty years ago: sparsely populated, mountainous, unspoiled. Bright and early Monday morning we set out with our suitcases and backpacks. Foolishly, I had overlooked the fact that it was rush hour. The first train was so full, we let it go by. Not even the white-gloved pushers could have wedged us into those cars. The next two were no less jammed, however. We decided to take an indirect route, a train circling the long way around, to Tokyo Station.

We managed to board one of these fairly easily and all was fine for a while, but as we got closer to our destination and the city's hub, the passenger count skyrocketed. We were packed in. All I could see was a wall of men's blue coats and women's white coats. Over the recorded thanks for riding the train and reminders to remember possessions, I called out a warning to Margo a few stations before our stop and we made a valiant effort to reach the doors with our luggage. After each stop we got a little closer, riding the shifts in the mass of people as it swelled in different directions. There was a kind of wave action to it. Then came Tokyo Station. I kept repeating that we were getting off and, in fact, we were carried to within a few steps of the car doors by the exiting surge of commuters, but then the reverse flow of passengers boarding hit us like a riptide. We were literally swept off our feet and carried back into the car. Helpless, we looked at each other as the train pulled out again. I signaled for us to inch toward the doors again so we could try one more to get off, but it was another two stops before we managed an escape.

"Well," said Margo, a little breathless. "That was cozy."

Mercifully, the train ride to Aizu-Wakamatsu was uneventful. To conserve our funds, we had planned to split a room. As Tohoku was the backwoods of Japan and therefore conservative, we thought it best to register as young marrieds. I took care of this at the local Green Hotel (a chain) and paid for the room. Wanting to square accounts before we lost track of the yen count, Margo reimbursed me for half the bill right there in the lobby. I thought nothing of it until I overheard a woman behind the desk telling her manager husband, "Strange, those foreigners. That man just made his wife pay for half their room."

We did some sightseeing and went to have dinner at a fabulous restaurant in a converted Japanese barn of traditional design. In the dining room, next to the rustic fireplace, was a couple with two precocious children who kept pointing at us and saying, "Look Daddy—foreigners! Gaijin, gaijin!"

After a while their father struck up a conversation and asked about our travels. I explained that we were touring Japan, that I had been in Japan for a year, on business, and that Margo had just joined me.

"Where are your children?" he asked, since most Japanese had children soon after marrying. I said we were on our honeymoon and the couple *oohed* and turned back to their meal, smiling.

Margo and I had almost finished dinner when the chef and an entourage of waiters and staff appeared bearing a huge platter of the fanciest dish on the menu.

The husband leaned over. "This is our honeymoon gift to you," he said, looking at us with real delight.

"What do we do now?" Margo said, smiling hard.

"We could throw the rice at each other," I said.

I thanked our benefactor, we had a few wedding toasts, and we ate and ate.

After our dining extravaganza, Margo and I ambled around the town until we came upon a *pachinko* parlor. I took her inside to show her this unique form of pinball and we sat down in front of a machine. We put in the necessary 100-yen coin and played the allotted fifteen balls. They were quickly gone and we slipped in another 100 yen, with similar results. Inexpert as we were, the coin slot was eating our money. We were about to stop when the man next to us motioned for us to wait. He left his stool and returned with a device that he stuck into our machine. It prevented the balls from disappearing: we could play forever. He put a coin in the slot and said, "Go ahead."

Margo and I played with abandon, our whoops and cries attracting the attention of the *sararimen* around us, all of them eyeing the crazy *gaijin*. When we were at last exhausted, we thanked the man profusely and, with much bowing, took our leave.

The next day it was the same story. Hearing we were newlyweds, the proprietor of a small pastry shop where we had stopped for some *imagawayaki* (pancakes with red bean paste) came running after us with a bag filled with more.

"Here," he said, "these are for you—a gift to the honeymoon travelers."

I thanked him for his generosity and began feeling a little guilty, though not enough to not enjoy the package of fresh, hot *imagawayaki*.

"You should be ashamed of yourself," Margo said, snatching a pancake from me and devouring it. "But why is it that everyone seems to focus on our marriage and children? Are they incredible romantics?"

"Hardly," I said, and held forth on the subject of marriage in Japan, while Margo snagged another *imagawayaki*.

Marriage and children were of paramount importance, but there was little emphasis on love—romantic love—except for maybe the honeymoon, which was why we were getting so much attention. Marriage, however, was entered upon to fulfill social obligations, maintain the proper image, and to maintain and enlarge the family's power. Traditional marriages were arranged by *omiai,* intermediaries. Even with so-called love matches becoming more common in urban areas, more than a third of city marriages were still arranged. In the countryside the matchmakers were kept even busier. A man was expected to wed by thirty-five, a woman by twenty-six. Children were conceived soon after the nuptuals.

Before marriage, during courtship, the woman was docile and solicitous. After marriage most became domestic tyrants and made all the major domestic decisions, raised the children, supervised their education, and took charge of their husbands' paychecks. This was the accepted norm.

"Very interesting," Margo said, her cheek smeared with red bean paste.

"Hey," I said, "all the pancakes are gone."

She feigned indignation. "Honeymooning is hard work. A girl's gotta eat."

●

We planned to catch the 6:30 train to Sendai after having dinner in the same restaurant we had reveled in the night before. Remembering us as the lovebirds from the previous evening, the staff ushered us into our own private room and served us a magnificent dinner, accompanied by two flasks of sake. By the time we remembered our schedule, our train was long gone. Fortunately there was another in forty-five minutes.

The restaurant had a taxi waiting for us and the entire staff bid us good-bye as we sped off to fetch our bags from the hotel desk and catch the final train. At the hotel there was a minor delay while they located the bags, although there shouldn't have been. The staff had clearly labeled them *gaijin*. Another farewell and we were rocketed to the station.

The train pulled in and we boarded, happy and tired, and I looked forward to a night's rest in Sendai. Except the train stopped at Koriyama. "I guess we transfer here," I said. Not so. It was this train's last stop, and there weren't any others until morning. We had to find shelter for the night and set off to hunt for a hotel. Of course, a few paces out of the station, we found ourselves in the usual red-light district. Ever the accommodations adventuress, Margo was anxious to add another type to her collection.

"How about it?" she said. "Are you game?"

I arched my eyebrows. What she meant was a love hotel, the Japanese version of a pay-by-the-hour no-tell motel. Margo had obviously studied up.

"Only twelve bucks and an outrageous experience," she said. "How can you resist?"

"Some of them are owned by Japanese mafia."

"So we can send out for some pizza. How do you feel about sausage and squid?"

We initiated our search with no success. "Just our luck," she said. "They're everywhere when you don't need them and now there's not a one in sight."

The touts lounging outside the bars and cabarets would know. I approached one barker, his hair slicked, shoes gleaming, and eyes hidden behind dark lenses. He nodded his answer to my request for directions and led us down a gaudy street. So there we were, following this sinister figure to nowhere that looked right. After a few blocks, he stopped in front of a bright white hotel, an obviously pristine and legitimate establishment and not at all what we had in mind. I asked him again. Comprehension dawned. He winked and resumed his guide duties.

Love hotels usually came in fantasy shapes, like castles, ocean liners, magical caves, and this was the sort of architecture I was looking for. Instead, he led us to a small office building, shut down for the night. Yet we were buzzed in and the barker led us to the third floor. A small sign announced we had arrived at the right sort of place. The man wished us a good time and was off into the night; we went to check in. The front desk consisted solely of a cashier's window; no indirection here. It was covered with opaque glass, with a small slot in which to slip money in exchange for keys. This helped maintain anonymity. Customers could use the facilities without worrying about having been seen, and the hotel people could honestly say they did not know who had been there if pressed by the constabulary or an irate spouse.

On the wall next to the cashier's window were descriptions and rates for the rooms available, some simple, some allegedly sumptuous. We opted for one of the latter, got our key, and marched up the hall. Room 7. It lived up to its billing. The motif was roughly Jules Verne, *Twenty Thousand Leagues Under the Sea*. Stalagtites descended from the ceiling, and stalagmites rose up from around the walls, which looked like sunken rock formations. There were murals, too: mermaids, Neptune with his trident, and a couple of angels thrown in for good measure. The floor was covered from wall to wall with cheap shag carpeting, and the bed was a giant clamshell. Margo tested the controls and made the bed rotate, elevate, and rock, hooting as it gyrated. It could have been a flying saucer. There was also a bar stocked with beer and a television. Margo popped open two cans and switched on the set. The offerings all seemed to be X-rated movies, and rather sadistic at that. Margo winced and, after a while, said, "I can't take any more of this." I didn't object and switched it off.

She was going to take the first shower, but saw that she had a problem. The bathtub was round, made of fake marble and rimmed with phony gold. It was also elevated, a nice touch. The bathroom wall was the problem. It was simply a huge pane of clear glass. "Kinky," she said.

"No problem," I insisted, "no problem." I would turn the clamshell bed around on its motorized base to face it away from the glass wall. A viable solution, except that when I did it, I realized the place was besotted with mirrors. No matter how you oriented anything, everything was visible from everywhere. By then Margo said she was too tired to do anything but collapse, so we got ready for bed, putting on our pajamas back to back.

"Margo," I said. "There's only one bed."

"You have a point."

"Yeah."

"Oh, well," she said. "It'll have to be the honor system. Everyone keep to his own side."

"Right," I said, and we got in. I switched off the light and settled down. But it was a little difficult to stay on your own side in a circular bed. Every time we started to drift off, our legs would slip out of bed, onto the floor. I clung to the edge and touched something next to it.

"Hey," she said, "was that an earthquake?"

"No," I said.

"I'm sure it was."

"I think I bumped the switches." The bed started rising and I groped for the button to stop it.

"It's a little late to be thinking about working on the transmission. Get us down!"

I pushed something else and the platform slowly spun.

"Are you playing our song or what? I'm beginning to feel like an LP, Gary."

"Sorry," I said, fumbling with switches. The bed stopped rotating and I flopped back, relieved.

"Hey," she said, "that wasn't a switch."

"Excuse me," I said, embarrassed. I was glad for the darkness so she couldn't see my flushed face.

"Oh, Gary-san," she said, yawning.

"What?" I said, utterly exhausted.

"I think you're wrong. I think . . . the earth . . . moved."

And then, ever so sweetly, she started to snore.

THIRTEEN

VULTURE SHOCK

W e awoke more tired than rested. The room was lightproof and we had slept late. By the time we got ourselves together and down to the desk to leave, it was ten o'clock. I tossed our key into the slot of the opaque cashier's window and we left, or tried to. A little old lady came chasing after us. In no uncertain terms, she lectured that after 9:00 A.M. the hourly meter started running again on the room, so we owed them a few dollars. I pretended not to understand but she was adamant, and I wondered if this was perhaps a mob-connected place. So I paid the extra fee and we left.

First by country train, all paneled in wood and looking like an ice cream parlor inside, and then by bus, we wended our way toward a resort in the mountains, a *rotenburo*, a hotel with an outdoor hot spring that Margo wanted to add to her collection of places. We were tight on time, though, and could only take a badly needed bath and make our next train connection.

The hotel was the standard gaudy affair. We paid a nominal fee at the desk for use of the hot springs and proceeded out the back, exiting at the top of a long flight of redwood stairs that descended into a gorge. The trees were budding, the last of the snow glistening beneath their boughs. A river roared in the distance. We could see its white water churning with spring runoff.

Margo took the lead and we walked down the steps—I counted about 280 of them—until we came to a wooden deck, just overlooking four steaming pools below it in the bathing area, each about twenty feet around. There were cubbyholes to the side of the deck and an old woman cleaning them.

"Uh, oh," I said.

Margo squinted in the sunlight. "What's the problem?"

"Mixed bathing," I said.

"Hey, this country just won't quit."

The cleaning lady was motioning toward the cubbyholes and saying we should leave our things there. She was urging us to disrobe and offering towels. We shifted around uncomfortably, stalling. The woman stared at us with a quizzical look, misunderstanding our hesitancy for concern about our luggage.

"No one will disturb anything," she said. "Your things will be safe here."

Margo said, "Tell her I'm a Republican, a Zoroastrian, anything!"

I said that we preferred to go down to the pools dressed. She shrugged and smiled, but I knew she must have thought us crazy. Margo didn't care; she was already walking down the last few steps to the bathing area.

I joined her at the bottom. It was a weekday morning so the place was deserted, but we still had our Western modesty to contend with.

"Well," she said, "are we going native or what?"

"Maybe you should go first, and then I'll go after."

"Not enough time if we're going to make the train, and there's no way we can go without."

"You're right," I said. We were both pretty scruffy. "Okay, maybe the steam will preserve our modesty."

Just then a breeze wafted through the gorge and dispersed the steam rising from the hot-spring waters.

"Yeah," she said, watching the mists part.

"Come on," I said, "be brave. It's broad daylight. The pools are four to five feet deep. We'll be submerged. We're in Japan. It's perfectly natural. This is the inscrutable, unrepressed Orient . . ." As I prattled on, we made our way to opposite sides of the area and stripped off our clothes. I heard a splash and peeked. Margo was in but bobbing around in reaction to the heat. "Keep still," I called out, "and you'll get used to it faster."

"*Don't* look!" she yelled.

"Forgot." Then I remembered I was standing there stark naked and leapt into the adjacent pool. Water and steam. "Oooh!" It wasn't that bad, but the difference between the air and water temperatures made it seem hotter.

I made myself settle down and let the water revive me. It was wonderful: the cleansing warmth, the smell of the minerals and the spring air, the light, the trees, and Margo's cherubic face in the pool next door.

"It's great, isn't it," I said, "once you're in."

"Mmm," she said, "and since you're a worldly gentleman, you can be the first one out."

I grimaced. "Can't we discuss this?"

"Nonnegotiable," she said, laughing.

●

The guidebooks touted the coastline of Matsushima as among the most beautiful places in Japan, so already I was leery of what we might find in so celebrated a place. It turned out that it was beauteous, with craggy cliffs, austere pine-covered islets, a sculpted bay, and clear blue water. It was also tawdry.

As we sailed through the bay aboard a sightseeing boat, the commentary coming over the public-address system ran non-stop, enlightening us about the depth of the ocean waters, their average temperature, the number of trees on each island. We were overjoyed to disembark. Alongside our craft lay another excursion boat at anchor, this one a gaudily painted Chinese dragon. The dockside telephone booths all had pagoda roofs. Margo gave me her let's-get-out-of-here look and we did.

That night, in a bar in Ichinoseki, she confessed that she had taken this holiday in Japan on a dare, but that she was beginning to think about possibly working here. I was about to disabuse her of this notion when a middle-aged man in white shirt and tie sat down next to us, introduced himself ("I am Dr. Ishikawa."), and initiated a conversation in English:

"I work at Sendai General Hospital. You've heard of it, haven't you? Yes, I'm a radiologist and I treat all the stars that come in with cancer," he said, and rattled off the names of many. He was obviously tipsy.

"You and my wife are in related fields," I said. "Margo works in computer graphics."

"What kind of computer graphics?" he said, addressing me.

"Ah, no," I said, "It's Margo, she works with computer graphics."

The good doctor continued to talk only to me. When he posed questions for her, he insisted on asking them through me.

It seemed as if he couldn't quite believe a woman could actually handle such work. Margo was incredulous. After our new acquaintance withdrew, she turned to me and said, "Is this typical insofar as attitudes about women?" I said that I was afraid it was representative and nearly universal. "So much for new horizons in Nippon. Come on, hubby, to our respective honeymoon beds."

The next day was Friday and we decided to rent a boat and take it down through Geibikei Gorge. The man at the boat rental said it was a slow day and offered, very generously, to be our guide and oarsman. He had dark, weathered skin, wore gray work clothes, a colorful headband, and high black boots — obviously an outdoorsman. We said yes. Out came paddles and a long pole. We hopped in and he started paddling. When he heard we were newlyweds, he became even more animated. "This is getting out of hand," Margo said, rolling her eyes.

Where the river grew shallow, our guide stood up and began punting. It was a rocky ride. Back in placid waters, he resumed paddling and said, "I would like to give you this as my wedding present," then he began to sing. It was a simple song but his melodic voice was startling: of operatic quality and enormous.

The boat floated along, as much on his voice as on the water, it seemed. We passed waterfalls and striking rock formations, the only humans on the river. Then, around the bend came a canoe. It was filled with Japanese men in blue suits and women dressed to the teeth. The women waved and the men aimed their cameras at us as our vessels passed in the middle of this virgin wilderness.

In the afternoon we had planned to visit some temples west of Ichinoseki, but the buses weren't running. It was the annual National Strike Day, when the railroad workers and all associated transport workers went out on their yearly strike. A regular occurrence, the strike was announced far in advance and would only last a day or two, except that this was the day.

We discussed the possibility of renting a car. Neither of us was up for driving Japanese fashion on the left-hand side, especially on these curvy roads. A taxi was what we needed, except that we couldn't find one.

Margo suggested we call one to come pick us up. I allowed as how that was a reasonable idea, if only we were able to read a telephone book. "Mmm," she said and we started walking. Presently we came to an elementary school, whose doors burst open as we neared, and a mob of children flew out, straight for us. They swarmed around us, pointing and shouting questions.

"What is your name?" "Where are you from?" "How old are you?" They yelled and jumped up and down. A few pressed close, holding up their baseball caps to show off the ensignias of various teams.

"We are Americans," I announced, "and we need your help."

"Ah," they said. "Do you know Michael Jackson?"

They were disappointed to hear we didn't but took it well. Still, one kid said, "Can you do the Moonwalk?" And another chimed in, "Yeah, like on the Su-re-er-a?"

Margo screwed up her face. " 'Su-re-er-a'?"

"Thriller," I said, and dug out some postcards of New York that I had been saving for an emergency. They went over big. I explained our predicament in calling a cab, gave one boy some money, and asked him to call us a taxi. He did.

We talked with them until the cab arrived, then said goodbye several dozen times as we pulled away. Streams of laughing, skipping children trailed out behind us and we waved some more.

•

Back in Tokyo, I found the door to my apartment open. Oh, no, I thought, and peeked in, expecting a shambles, my worldy possessions looted. Instead there was perfect order: everything vacuumed, the bed made with fresh sheets and turned down. Apparently the *gaijin* mansion's bimonthly maid had forgotten to lock up.

Margo was deeply impressed with how safe Japan seemed to be. I told her the crime rate was nil and that most police did not even carry weapons. Until fairly recently there had not even been a word in Japanese for lock.

After she had checked in at a nearby inn, we attended a *hanami*, a cherry blossom viewing, outside the Emperor's Palace. A traditional gathering, its ostensible purpose was to celebrate the evanescence of beauty. In reality, the *hanami* were wild, boisterous celebrations with a great deal of singing and drinking and dancing. As reserved as the Japanese were most of the time, at an occasion like this they really let loose. Men were dancing with women, men with men, women with women.

We wandered among the revelers, watching the merriment and dodging raucous celebrants. Every few feet we would pass a group sitting on a blanket and we would be invited to sit down and join them. Finally we gave in and joined a group of a dozen *sararimen*. All were wearing dark blue suits, Margo pointed out, a sign she interpreted as indicating they were a safe risk. I pointed out that they were not wearing their shoes, but she gave me a puzzled look and obviously did not read anything into this.

The men were definitely in an informal mode. They offered us beer and dried squid and sang songs. Some were curious and asked oddly pointed questions. Trotting out yet again our newlyweds ploy, I hoped for the sort of near reverential responses we had gotten all along. Instead, one of the men commented on Margo's good looks and asked for our phone number, intimating that he would be glad to call whenever I was away on business. Another made a crack about "honeymoon children" and another said in English: "Go for it!"

Margo drew closer. Unfortunately, the group's manager chose this moment to leave, and a couple of the men became even more animated about their feelings for Margo. She gave them a rictus smile and we left, too. As we strolled about, I tried to explain that the Japanese took Western films and such literally when it came to women. In fact, one guidebook had printed on its inside cover a rebuff in Japanese. A woman could hold it in front of her for the aggressor to study.

"Or walk around holding it in front of her, kind of like a wreath of garlic?" Margo said.

"Something like that," I replied.

The *hanami* was the last of our tourism. Margo was going home. We walked from the train station toward my apartment, past the *obento* take-out shops and the usual caravan that appeared each evening of *yatai* or "night stands," each vending quick meals. Their vapors mingled as we passed: noodles in soup, fried noodles, *takoyaki* (octopus in pancake butter), *oden* (fish and vegetables in a broth dabbed with hot mustard).

We had our farewell meal in a *yatai* booth. Margo gave me a hug and said, "It's been a wonderful marriage, darling, and I must say something to you."

"Yes," I said, puffing up a bit in expectation of hearing my virtues extolled.

"I want a divorce," she said.

FOURTEEN

THEORY ZZZZZZZZZZZ

The commute out to CSK was ninety minutes each way. As always, directions were difficult, there being no guideposts I recognized, no geographical information, no street names, no sequential house numbers. Still, I thought I had gotten everything except, naturally, the most vital item: the name of the train station where I was to get off.

It had sounded like Gesha Eki, meaning Gesha Station, only I could not find it on the map. I asked my fellow commuters. They listened, stared, then shrugged. No one seemed to know what I was talking about. Luckily, I remembered mention of a Takashimaya department store branch, and when one came into view as we pulled into a station, I hopped off.

After attempting to find the place on my own, I called in. A rescue team of three came to fetch me and showed me to CSK. They were much amused by my trouble in finding Gesha Station.

"Gesha Eki is not the name of the station," one of the gentlemen explained. "It means, 'the station where you get off.'" No wonder the other passengers had looked at me so oddly.

The company was in the middle of Futagotamagawaen, a residential suburban area that bordered a rural district, so there were homes and farms and country roads surrounding us. I was ushered in and met in the lobby by an Office Lady who presented me with slippers to wear in the building. Upstairs I met Yoneda-san, my immediate superior, and his staff of five. They all stood there in their three-piece suits and slippers. As they handed me their business cards, they bowed and introduced themselves.

None of the other staff members understood English, Yoneda-san informed me, so we spoke in Japanese about my first assignment: to help design a research institute. He would provide me with background articles and papers in English. Yoneda-san reminded me of my division manager at Sony. His autocratic air was not unfamiliar. No bottom-up decision process here. He called the shots, disregarding everyone else. An invitation was extended for me to live in the company's dormitory, a two-hour commute each way. I declined, with thanks.

Over the next week I waited for the background file and got to know the company and my fellow workers. It was, I could see, even more conservative than Sony in some ways. Of the 3,500 employees, only one woman held a position other than that of an Office Lady. Whereas at Sony we had been off most Saturdays, at CSK half a day's work was mandatory every Saturday. There were also some impressive daily rituals.

Every morning all the employees held group meetings before work and participated in the regular routine. First, everyone practiced bowing, and repeated in unison the same phrases:

"Good morning. Good morning. Good morning. . . . I will

take care of it. I will take care of it. . . . I am sorry. I am sorry. . . . Good-bye. Good-bye. . . ."

These were said repeatedly until everyone had achieved the proper intonation and conveyed the right degree of respect. Then a group member got up and gave a rousing pep talk, summoning us to work and sacrifice, and led us in the company song. The firm's anthem praised the corporation and expressed our pride and devotion.

I recognized the melody as the theme song from *Flashdance*. A single loud clap by the group signaled the conclusion. An abbreviated version of the morning ritual served as the closing ceremonies at the end of the day.

As at Sony, the younger workers thought the daily rallies were meaningless but did not voice their skepticism for fear of being ostracized. They said they felt silly singing the company song yet there was little choice. The older employees, they thought, liked the ceremonies and were genuinely enthusiastic, although I wondered if this was not perhaps a simple rationalization.

Yoneda-san invited me to dinner at his home on Sunday, and I was glad for the opportunity to be with him in an informal setting. An American colleague was also in town and would be joining us, he informed me when I arrived. The house, I was curious to see, was decorated and furnished Western-style and we sat on chairs at the dinner table. Dinner was a sushi and sashimi buffet. Yoneda-san proudly told us his wife had prepared it all herself. Like a good Japanese housewife, she did not eat with us but remained in the kitchen.

The assortment of food on the table was vast and I stuffed myself like a good guest, as Yoneda-san insisted. Even though we tried to politely decline refills, he would plunk more on our plates. I wasn't surprised. It was the Japanese custom to insist even after food has been declined. The resistance and insistence constituted a delicate dance. It was proper for the host to press more food upon guests, given the general unwillingness of Japanese to ask for something outright and thereby risk appearing selfish. Even so, guests normally expressed reluctance to accept a second portion as it was tantamount to taking food away from the rest of the group. But if the host puts the food on the guests' plates, the guest is absolved of all responsibility.

Sometimes, like me, the guest really doesn't want more, but not eating what is on your plate is intolerably rude, so I ate . . . and ate.

●

Determined to maintain the few friendships I had made at Sony, I telephoned Maruyama-san and Kondo-san to let them know how I was doing. They sounded uncomfortable. I attributed it to the lack of privacy in their offices and the company's strict policy about personal calls. So I suggested their calling me at home, or vice versa. Neither offered their home numbers.

I also wanted to keep up with Takagi-san, someone whose sincere friendship I had never doubted, yet he was never around when I rang, nor did he return any of my messages. Stubbornly, I pressed them for a dinner foursome and managed to arrange a mutually convenient date. But when the evening arrived, only Maruyama-san met me. The others couldn't make it, she said, but sent their regards. The evening was stiff and awkward, with constant references to Sony as her company and CSK as mine. It was the last time I would see her.

Situations determined behavior. Situations delineated friendship, and not feelings. I knew that to be very Japanese. Still . . .

As luck would have it, I ran into two other Sony colleagues
coming home one evening. We exchanged greetings; as I
started to describe my new job they excused themselves
abruptly and quickly left. Not long afterward the same thing
occurred with some other people I knew from Sony. It was
painfully self-evident that they were no longer willing to associate with me now that I was an outsider. The corroboration by
these acquaintances somehow stirred up what I had not wanted
to think about my former office pals at Sony. Intellectually, I
knew it was a cultural thing with them, yet it hurt nonetheless.

Back at work, I went to see Yoneda-san and asked after the
articles and papers he had promised. Yoneda-san just stared. A
Japanese employee would never have reminded him of his earlier promise to deliver the material. He would have waited
patiently and accepted the situation, whatever the outcome.

Yoneda-san said nothing. I knew Japanese fell silent when
uncomfortable. He was indicating that he knew he had done
wrong but wasn't about to admit it. Being Japanese meant never
having to say you're sorry, except, ironically, when you hadn't
done anything for which to apologize. Then profuse apologies
were the norm. People apologized for nothing: for finishing a
box of cookies, for appearing for dinner on time—"I apologize
for interrupting you."—for someone else stepping on their feet.
It was for the innocent party to assume responsibility for the
other person's feelings, but if a superior made a mistake, he
never apologized.

Yoneda-san no doubt noted my tone, my tense face, and rigid
posture. However, it took two to tangle and he wasn't about to,
so he didn't say a thing. Trying to argue with a Japanese was like
fighting a pillow: you simply got no resistance. Yoneda-san

preferred to remain mute and not lose face. The stoney silence was so thick it seemed to have substance.

He was taking responsibility for my feelings as well. Anger constituted a loss of control, and therefore was an embarrassing loss of face. By maintaining his hard silence, Yoneda-san not only saved face, at the same time he avoided an unpleasant conflict that might have harmed our relationship. In that sense, he helped me save face, too. I didn't feel grateful, just disappointed. I wasn't being paid by CSK so perhaps I wasn't really a part of CSK. Certainly there was no incentive to keep me productively engaged.

After Takahashi-san returned from a business trip, I explained the situation. He sidestepped Yoneda-san's inability to facilitate my work on the first project. "Shikata ga nai," he said. It can't be helped. And he suggested I begin work on the second project with someone who definitely spoke English. This was a software system to be marketed from the more centrally located office in Shinjuku. He himself would be away again the following week, but I could introduce myself and start on it right away.

The commute to Shinjuku was much shorter and much more uncomfortable. I had been traveling opposite to the rush hour flow. Now I was commuting at the height of the rush hour into the city's prime commuter destination. Shinjuku Station was not only Tokyo's but the country's busiest, used by millions of people each and every day as they struggled to reach their workplaces among the district's skyscrapers. Even at the quietest hours it was continually busy, the cadre of ticket punchers continuously sending up a cacophonous chatter as they invalidated tickets.

Each morning the cars were jammed with laborers, blue-suited men and gray-attired women. Uniformed, white-gloved transit men worked as "pushers" to attain the maximum yield from each car. The trains were filled to capacity and then added to by the pushers jamming stray limbs and backsides into the mass of humanity wedged into each car. And everyone was in a mad rush—to catch buses, trains, elevators, all ticking like the clocks that governed their schedules and physical motions throughout the day.

The trains were incredible: passengers mashed together. People who would apologize profusely for the slightest inadvertent contact here were cheek to jowl. In the anonymity of the impossible density *chikans* marauded, groping women. The same respectable men who bowed politely and made all varieties of courteous gestures, took advantage of the crush and young women's silent embarrassment to molest. And everywhere a hand might actually be raised there appeared the lurid *manga* comics.

At the Shinjuku office I introduced myself and inquired after the second project. The equipment for it had not yet arrived; there was nothing to do. I would have another couple of weeks to read newspapers and study Japanese. I also decided to do some investigating of Japanese business methods and economics, since I had time on my hands. Shikata ga nai.

●

The goal I posed for myself was to test the veracity of all those glowing American business books on Japan, the awed tones of business articles in our magazines and newspapers, and the adulatory lectures I had dutifully listened to in school, all touting the efficiency of their inventory systems, the country's full employment, job security, consensus building, quality circles. . . . What was the truth?

After seeing what workers had to put up with, I was no longer confident that the "lifetime employment" that many Westerners thought Japanese received was a benefit or a liability. Now I knew that it was not even uniformly true, much less positive or negative. In reality, only those who worked for large corporations were guaranteed this, and they were nearly all men. The major firms accounted for about 30 percent of the total work force. Women, part-time workers, the working retired, and the workers in small companies—70 percent of the labor force—had no such guarantee.

On closer examination, even the third who did have, didn't really. Japanese were forced to retire at age fifty-five. Since the pension and social security systems were woefully inadequate, people had to continue to work to simply support themselves. Some stayed on in their companies, although with less responsibilities and diminished salaries. More often they went to work for firms that supplied the parent company. Or they learned a trade or craft and worked at a lower salary in a cottage industry. So, full employment and lifetime employment did not apply to all of one's productive years.

The celebrated low unemployment figures, I concluded, were also misleading. The Japanese calculated their numbers differently and their approach was intended to keep the unemployment totals artificially deflated. This was achieved in a number of ways.

True, workers might not be laid off during economic slowdowns, as they were in the United States, but Japanese workers were consistently required to accept fewer hours or lower wages. Also, part-time employees, a very large segment of the work force, were always counted as fully-employed workers. Even when their already abbreviated hours and wages were further reduced during a slack period, they remained in the tally of the fully employed. Likewise, the employee who retired at fifty-five, and usually took on part-time work or a lesser-paying job, was not included in the unemployment figures. Many hidden workers were also omitted, such as unpaid family members toiling in a small shop or restaurant, as was commonplace in Japan. With so many retailers and cottage industries comprising so much of Japan's business community, this number could not be insignificant. National unemployment figures simply did not factor in all the facts, and deliberately overlooked a number of segments in the adult population. The methods of measurement did not match the structure of the economy: The numbers were misleading.

So was the confidence professed by employees of large firms in never being laid off in the event of economic downswings. Everyone at Sony, for instance, maintained that it had never happened and just could not happen. Due to the country's extraordinary growth rate over the past forty years, there had never been a recession so severe that layoffs were called for. Further, the paternalistic attitude of firms simply would not permit such measures.

I pretty much accepted this at face value, as it reinforced what I had already read about Japanese corporate practices in the course of my studies. What they did not tell me was that these very same companies who profess such policies do, however, pass along their financial woes to the vast network of subcontractors that service them. In point of fact, large Japanese firms do not manufacture their own parts. Ancillary companies produce these and then ship the parts to the large firm, which operated like a giant assembler. Since there were thousands of different components used daily by firms like Sony, the network was necessarily huge. As each individual vendor usually supplied a single large company exclusively, it was locked into the economic policies dictated by that giant firm. It was these vendors who had to cut their profit margins, accept fewer orders, lower workers' hours or salaries, and even lay off employees, while the firm they serviced maintained a pristine no-layoffs policy.

This dovetailed with another myth about the Japanese economic miracle. Japanese companies prided themselves on maintaining reduced inventories and thereby holding down costs, as evident in their laudable balance sheets. The truth, however, was not as clear-cut, because while the large companies basked in this example of their efficiency, subcontractors absorbed the carrying costs for the waiting inventory and virtually acted as warehouses for the larger companies. Being small, these suppliers could not produce large quantities on demand and therefore maintained large stores of parts in order to fulfill orders when they did materialize. To offset the negative effect of carrying such inventories, they paid lower salaries and offered few or no benefits. Despite this, the Western press insisted on perpetuating the myth of the Japanese inventory system's efficiency—and the myth of Japan as a nation with full employment. The poorly protected and poorly paid subcontractors' employees made me think twice about accepting the conventional thinking on the subject.

Of all the virtues of Japanese management that had been preached in business school, the concern for human sensibilities, the worker's sense of participation, and improved productivity were the most highly touted, while the short-term goals and profit priorities of American managements were severely criticized and blamed for all varieties of business woes. The Japanese emphasis on a content and responsible worker was singled out in texts as the chief reason for their economy's success. This was evidenced by their consensus-building, bottom-up decision making, their lifetime employment guarantees, medical services, company subsidized cafeterias, and dormitory accommodations. I was now much more skeptical about all of these unquestioned truths and the overall strength of their corporate structures. It seemed patently obvious to me that American publishers and media had glossed over the social and psychological costs of the allegedly benign Japanese system. The Japanese economic miracle seemed to have much more to do with the Zen-like discipline and selflessness of the work force than any innovativeness in corporate management.

How many Western writers actually spoke Japanese or spent more than a few weeks doing their on-site research? How many had simply repeated what the Japanese interpreted their economy to be like? The Japanese, ever anxious about saving face and hiding their shortcomings, had provided the right cosmetic data. How many researchers obtained their information firsthand, as opposed to culling the academic and popular press for their insights? A reading knowledge of the Romance languages or German is common; a reading knowledge of Japanese is not. Not surprisingly then, far less has been translated from Japanese into other languages than vice versa. Prohibitively high living expenses further limited access by foreign students, businessmen, and travelers. Our graduate schools welcomed Japanese students; the reverse was not true, although the Japanese were suddenly being enormously generous about subsidizing Japanese studies by American universities. Considerable funds were being allocated for the forging of ties and creating an image, a public perception. How critically would these underwritten studies evaluate Japanese culture, history, and business?

All of this compounded our ignorance about Japan and sometimes even disinformed us. Even information under our noses was insufficiently examined. Of the 238 businesses in the

United States owned by Japanese in 1981, 20 were employing the revered quality circles common throughout Japanese companies. American workers resisted wearing uniforms and even company hats, opting instead for their union headgear.

Certainly, I was convinced that what I was seeing in Japan would not succeed in the United States. More and more, the adaptations of Japanese corporate approaches and techniques by Western managers seemed like the fruitless pursuit of fad diets. They wouldn't ultimately work for Americans, and maybe did not even work so well for the Japanese, judging from their comparatively low standard of living, woefully inadequate social services, civic facilities, housing, and retirement systems. The individual mattered very little in the overall development of national economic power, except as an interchangeable unit. The cogs made whatever sacrifices were called for, the group's strength was paramount. Why else would the tiniest public mention of individualism strike such fear into the hearts of Japanese economists, as it so obviously did.

The Japanese middle class, especially its younger members, were changing. I thought it remarkably telling that they had to go outside their own language (with its fourteen different words for "you") and bring into it the means of voicing their different sense of themselves. Standing beside his white automobile, the thirty-year-old company man would express his newfound pride in possession by saying, in Japanese, a recently coined word: *Mycar!*

•

The good news was that my Japanese was finally good enough for me to carry on conversations in everyday language. It made life so much easier and enjoyable, although sometimes it also made people think I was more conversant than I actually was, and I would quickly find myself in over my head.

The bad news was that my Japanese was so much better that it made many people nervous. People I addressed wouldn't respond and insisted instead on speaking to me in English, even when my Japanese was unquestionably better than their English. It was a resistance that longtime foreign residents had warned me would occur once my skills improved. Such mastery, they theorized, was disquieting and invasive, threatening their native belief in their own cultural uniqueness and superiority. It was as if they prided themselves in their culture and language being too difficult for anyone else to understand. They were actually disconcerted if you spoke too well.

So instead of going out more among ordinary Japanese, I found myself back at the CommInn speaking English. There I met a young Japanese woman who seemed oddly familiar. I couldn't place her and kept staring at the modern haircut and opalescent dark eyes. Her English was excellent; we chatted. I found myself discussing art, American films, and Passover.

"Passover?" I said, incredulous. Most Japanese I had met thought Judaism was a branch of Christianity. I was dumbfounded that she had even heard of Passover.

"You're Jewish aren't you?" she said. "What can you tell me about Passover?"

After three-quarters of an hour it finally came to me that we had met before, although she seemed so different this time.

"My name is Setsuko," she said, and confessed that we had met once before, at Saburo-san's party. The somewhat resentful Office Lady who had been so haughty when I'd asked her for her card.

"Can I have your card again?" I said.

"Are you sure you want it?" she said, very seriously.

"Yes. And I'll call."

She gave me her card and I did call, making a date with her for Sunday. As agreed, I met her at Gotanda Station. She seemed to have softened and smiled more. From behind her back she produced a bouquet of pink carnations.

"For your birthday."

She had found out Friday had been my birthday.

"Is pink okay?" she asked, worried that I might think the color feminine.

"They're beautiful," I said, "like you."

We had tea and talked. What she wanted to know about most was the Talmud, of all things. I had to laugh. There I was, ten thousand miles from home, sitting in the middle of Tokyo talking about holy writ.

"And if it is defiled, violated—"

"Desecrated," I said.

"Yes. Then you hold a funeral for it?" she said.

I nodded. "If it has basically been destroyed, yes. It is considered a living entity to be mourned and buried with proper ritual."

We talked for hours. She wanted to know why men didn't shave when somebody died and why the mirrors were covered at times of grieving, and why Jews were forbidden on certain holidays to tear things, even toilet paper. How she was incorporating all this discussion of biblical history and beliefs into her cultural framework I could not even guess, but she was well versed and interested.

Later in the week I was invited to a party at a law firm and invited Setsuko. Afterward we went to a *kissaten* for dessert and coffee and talked about a former American boyfriend of hers. The place closed and we went on to another. Some time after eleven o'clock it closed, too. I suggested we call it a night.

"I live in Saitama prefecture," she said, "and the last train has already departed."

"Ah, I know a capsule hotel near my apartment. Maybe you could stay there."

Setsuko did not say anything.

"Or . . . you could . . . you could spend the night . . . with me."

"That is very kind of you," she said, very softly. "Thank you, very much."

•

The few evenings out I had ever spent with Japanese women, I noticed they had been extremely careful to steer us toward restaurants with international clientele. On a few occasions I had noted the rueful asides of other patrons—other Japanese—obviously displeased to see a Japanese dining alone with a *gaijin*. On one occasion a very cosmopolitan young woman, who had lived abroad and was completely fluent in English, joined me for dinner, chatting easily and using American slang. However, when we later accidentally ran into some of her friends, she turned completely cold and, in very patronizing Japanese, passed me off as a sort of stray pet upon whom she had taken pity. Being out alone with a male colleague was unacceptable behavior for a female employee. Being out alone with a foreigner, I gathered, was compromising no matter what the circumstances. The vehemence of the reactions to Setsuko and myself in public were startling for their rudeness.

Seeing her home one evening on the train, she rested her head on my shoulder, and we incurred the wrath of our fellow passengers. Snide comments, nasty looks—the most innocent contact seemed to prompt a near outcry. That we were romantically involved was something for us to be wary of, something we needed to remember not to give away or in any way demonstrate publicly, or we would be subjected to verbal abuse. Then again, the verbal abuse took place even if we were simply together. Even taking a meal together would often become an ordeal, except perhaps in the larger restaurants catering more to foreign patrons. So I was not surprised when she suggested we go once again to the Lion Beer Hall in the Ginza. It was a Japanese version of a German beer garden and prided itself on serving the best approximation of Wienerschnitzel in Tokyo.

Setsuko's family was not pleased either, she told me, and she was careful to mislead her parents as to her true whereabouts whenever she spent the night at my place. Each time she would call home and say she was staying with a girlfriend. One Friday when she called home, her mother told her the company had called.

"Something important?" I asked, expecting to hear of some business crisis.

"No," she said. "Firms will often call the homes of single young women on Friday night on some pretext. They're checking to make sure we are safely tucked in at a reasonable hour and not off somewhere endangering their corporate image."

"Are you serious . . . bedchecks? They called to make sure you were home? A corporate curfew?"

She nodded. "A company's reputation rests on that of its employees. If its employees have questionable reputations, they must be put back in line. That is the philosophy. It is ridiculous but that is the way things are here. And if one family member is discovered to be disreputable or disloyal to the company in some way, then it is a mark against everyone related to him or her. If a woman's whereabouts are suspect, or if one explores the possibility of a job in another firm, this is noted, the record preserved. It can affect the careers of all of the person's relatives."

I now realized the other tension I sensed in her when we were out in public: She was constantly on guard, fearful that someone from the firm might see her with me. As a result, we stayed in more, or went to exceptionally public places, like baseball parks, where the odds were more in our favor and the setting was less intimate than a restaurant.

Moving about Tokyo with Setsuko opened my eyes to what life was like for a woman in Japanese society. It did not look appealing. Basically, you had to be someone you weren't. You could not smoke in public, not in the street or even at your desk at the office. You could not drink or go out unchaperoned.

Single women were required to live at home, to submit to checks upon their personal behavior. They were grudingly educated and minimally trained once employed; their career prospects steadily diminished by the age they were expected to be married and gone from major firms, and after which they could expect little or nothing by way of challenging work or further advancement. Most women left and accepted less pay from smaller companies, which explained to me the nearly universal female work forces in some of the service companies I had dealt with, like the all-female outfit that provided my Japanese tutor.

Most women accepted their traditional wife-mother role and assumed the primary power in the family. But still, I wanted to know, wasn't the rigidity of their restricted lives frustrating? Even if they controlled the family's finances and all, weren't they unhappy with their lot, weren't they terribly lonely? Setsuko allowed as how many were but was reluctant to elaborate.

What did these women do while their husbands worked all day and partied most nights? Setsuko sighed, hearing my question.

"They read *manga,* go shopping, think about suicide, become shrews, or turn to swallows," she said in Japanese.

"Swallows? I don't follow."

"Swallows—young men. They take younger lovers while their husbands are out, cavorting around or working late or golfing or whatever."

Eventually Setsuko's parents found out about us. They were displeased that their grown daughter was not always home at night. What was worse was that she was involved with a *gaijin.* What exactly was the upsetting thing for them, I wanted to know. It took some prodding for Setsuko to tell me. She said that if her parents' families, or their neighbors and friends, found out about us, her mother and father would be held responsible for her unacceptable behavior and they would all be ostracized. No one in Setsuko's neighborhood had ever been involved with a foreigner.

It was not simple exclusion. There was, in the Japanese attitude toward *gaijin,* an implicit superiority, but then I suppose racial superiority is inherent in discrimination.

The phone rang one Friday evening and I answered. It was Setsuko's mother. I had never spoken to her but of course knew that my reputation preceded me. I waited for some sort of verbal assault or displeased tone at least. Instead she gave a common socially dictated response often heard when someone has aided another member of the speaker's family. Setsuko's mother thanked me for what I had done for her daughter: helping her with her computer programming skills. This was proper etiquette and she was a proper Japanese mother. Despite her feelings about me, she maintained the appropriate social form. Despite her propriety, the message was clear. Unless you were born Japanese, you would always be outside and at some point you would experience discrimination—rejection.

Some tension developed between myself and Setsuko for a number of reasons. She was so totally compliant that it was maddening: Anything I wanted to do was wonderful, anyplace I wanted to go was lovely, anything I wanted to eat, see, buy, rent, visit. Likewise, the instant she arrived at my place, she would set about cleaning, tidying, straightening. It was very proper behavior for a Japanese woman but unbearably servile as well. Everything said and done was to please the male and nothing was, for certain, honestly felt or desired or thought. Even in the most intimate matters, technique seemed to be all. The universal Japanese obsession with it was relentless. Form was everything.

Setsuko grew aloof, distant. When I asked her about it, I did not hear what I thought I would — a litany of my shortcomings, failings, cultural blindspots.

Instead she said, "I must be careful, yes. After all, you are a foreigner."

FIFTEEN

LESSONS FOR AMERICA

Disaster struck in the form of a cold. A minor thing in the West, I feared it could be major trouble where I was, because in Japan you simply don't stay out sick. A rare sick day might be managed if one's record were unblemished, but two sick days was an unpardonable breach of loyalty. I was just sick enough to miss two and lay there fevered and miserable about their possibly seeing it as a lack of commitment (not that I had any work yet to commit to). The last thing I wanted was to cause problems by my absence. To make things even worse, I had prepared a marketing plan for an artificial intelligence project but had missed the meeting because of my cold. When I returned to the office, Takahashi-san said there was no point in reading it now. Then I knew they were holding the sick days against me. Once violated, their trust was not easily recouped.

Yoneda-san must have sensed my resignation. To cheer me up, he started buying me lunch and referring to me as "special guest of honor." The evening he invited a group of us out to dinner, everyone sat nervously fidgeting with their menus. I had seen this behavior before, at Sony one night when a higher up joined us after work. Tonight was a replay: Once Yoneda-san had placed his order, everyone placed theirs for the exact same dish. That way no one would stand out and no possible offense could be taken for deviating from the boss's or the group's decision.

Yoneda-san had me sit in on job interviews, although I could not understand or follow most of them. When his subordinates were done with their questions, I was prevailed upon to pose one in English to test the applicants' verbal skill. It was such an obviously token function that the applicants usually answered me in Japanese.

Still, I appreciated Yoneda-san's efforts in trying to make me feel part of the group. His intentions were kind, no doubt, but I wanted more. I wanted to work. Instead, I now saw that I was only there for *imeji*. America was where artificial intelligence was happening. Having an American on board would bring the firm prestige. Yoneda-san showed me off to job applicants, venture capitalists, and potential customers—anyone he wished to impress—in hopes that having an American member of the firm would attract funds or business. Since I never said much at any of these encounters, my possible contributions were obviously irrelevant. My symbolic importance was what mattered. I was so much window dressing.

I couldn't see the point of it and decided to leave CSK. I called the Asia Foundation to say I wouldn't be staying on there. Mr. Morton shot back that he was ordering my plane tickets home, that I should plan to leave the country by the end of the week. Having learned my lessons in indirection, I called Takahashi-san at CSK and told him that if he was interested in keeping me, he had better call Mr. Morton. He did.

Mr. Morton rang me back promptly, saying: "Don't worry

about a thing. CSK had wonderful things to say about you. Keep up the good work." So back I went.

There was another project that went nowhere but I did get drafted to advise the firm on the advanced training of their staff at American universities. Then Kawamura-san, the general manager of their International Division, heard I was idle and asked me to work for him on a project involving telecommunications. I was joyous. And the man spoke perfect English to boot.

The project involved canvassing American companies in Tokyo. We were to determine their telecommunication needs. So I would call the various companies and make inquiries. Usually a few minutes on the phone was enough to establish whether a meeting was warranted. Kawamura-san, however, set up a meeting with a company I had determined was not interested. He knew it, too. We made the crosstown trip anyway. The American company still wasn't interested.

Several other useless trips ensued, including a long and complicated journey involving no small number of trains and a couple of cabs. When we finally arrived, we were introduced to our hosts in order of our eminence as we exchanged business cards. Once everyone knew everyone else's place in the hierarchy, then the proper level of language and other deferential considerations could be appropriately adjusted. Unfortunately, the person we were hoping to see was not in that day, nor was he even in town. A phone call confirming this would have obviously saved a colossal waste of six people's time, I thought.

Our hosts provided us with a substitute with whom we exchanged formalities and drank coffee for forty-five minutes. Then it was back into the cabs and trains.

Why had six people lost an afternoon of work? I finally asked Kawamura-san about the wild-goose chases.

He said, "Before a Japanese will enter into a business relationship, he wants to know the people he may be dealing with. This requires the investment of time. Even though a particular person is not interested now, perhaps after three or four visits to his office and a few evenings out, drinking and eating, a relationship can be established. Sales will eventually follow."

"I see," I said. "Please go on."

"In the short run no sales will be generated. But once some personal bonds are in place, sales will flow freely, sometimes more because of the relationship itself than from any cost or product advantages. Once you reach that stage, gaining sales becomes as easy as calling an old friend."

The project was concluded and nothing else substantive was in the offing. I went to Yoneda-san to formally withdraw from the company.

To my surprise, he seemed genuinely concerned. "You shouldn't leave! There is more than enough English in the office. We just have not exploited the full potential." The discussion moved from his immediate work area out into the open bullpen of desks. In front of everyone he announced, "I am willing to speak more English, and the staff is all good in English and would relish this opportunity to hone their skills."

The staff looked on half amazed and half horrified, volunteering nothing.

"Yes," Yoneda-san said, seconding himself. "All you have to do is say yes and we will all live as one big happy family. Yes?"

I smiled and said nothing, having learned by now that it would be amusing but impolite to point out that the boss had said all this in Japanese.

I had two chance encounters before I left Japan that were interesting and, personally, more. The first was with the director of the Japan Society's intern program, which was similar to that of the Luce Foundation. "Don't fret," he said, "and don't blame yourself. Your experience was to be expected from the outset. For the past six summers I have placed American MBA candidates in large Japanese companies so they could learn about Japanese management. Their experiences were just like yours. Even though the companies promised to open their doors, they never gave the interns any meaningful work or exposure. Year after year the interns come to me grumbling about the companies' unwillingness to open up."

The second encounter was on a train two days before my scheduled departure and a few days after my being interviewed in an English-language magazine. A woman, a Westerner, approached me and exclaimed, "You don't know how happy you've made me! You know, I'm glad someone else has the same feelings as I do about working as a *gaijin* in a Japanese company. For so long I thought my experiences so crazy, and my feelings toward the Japanese so irrational and extreme, that I assumed it was me."

●

Japanese children commonly slept in their parents' beds until the age of four or five or six. It made for tremendous emotional bonding and accounted perhaps for lifelong difficulties with separation that took the form of a pervasive fear that carried into adult life. To be ostracized, or to be left, was ineffably painful. If one added to that the cultural prohibition against expressing emotion, it made leaving someone an oddly unfinished process.

Most of my partings were classically Japanese. One friend said good-bye as if I would see him the next day, even though we might never meet again. Another separated from me in a crowd as we left the restaurant after our last dinner together, then waved good-bye as he disappeared down the subway stairs.

Setsuko kept it jolly and added her going-away gift to my growing collection.

"Oh, it's beautiful," I said. "But what is it?"

She laughed. "Japanese pajamas. Do you like the color?"

"Yes," I said, "I adore pink."

And then, of course, there was our Fourth of July farewell dinner at the Nishiyamas. I left my shoes at the door and presented Mrs. Nishiyama with perfectly wrapped flowers. Joel and the others were already there. As I entered, I thanked her for her hospitality and she complimented me on my Japanese.

At dinner, Mrs. Nishiyama brought forth a bountiful tray of seaweed, rice, and fish for sushi rolls. I took tiny portions. As soon as any of us finished, she put more on our plates with customary aplomb.

Afterward Joel and Taro took their clarinets from the waiting cases next to the baby grand and Mr. Nishiyama turned on the recorder. They played beautifully the same pieces they had played at each previous gathering. When they finished, I was prevailed upon to once again play my piano repertory of original compositions while the camera flashed and clicked.

Toward the evening's end farewell gifts were presented to each of us. We each received a red, white, and blue *hapi* coat decorated with pictures of Martians celebrating the Tsukuba World's Fair. We also each accepted a calligraphy set, complete with delicate brushes and fine paper, the same writing tools used in Nippon for thirteen centuries.

I thought about the sense of ritual and meditation at Japanese meals, the silence while eating, the arrangement of food on a plate. Joel and I had once talked about how Parisian Tokyo was in some respects, how French its sewers, how form and appearance conscious its citizens. But now I saw Japan as more British, more imperial. Joel's superior at the hospital had once exclaimed that Japan was not the East. I now partly understood what he had meant. It was not Asia in the way England was not Europe. It saw itself as standing apart, alone and different from its neighbors.

Listening to the conversations at the table, I picked up my tea. The mug had no handle and required me to hold it in both hands. I savored the warmth, as the potter had intended, felt the texture of the irregular glaze. How many evenings had I boiled my body, donned a thin cotton robe, and gently eased toward sleep in my fresh futon.

Like the night I had gotten lost on the way back to the dormitory and only managed to crawl into my room a few hours before dawn, exhausted. I had lain there in the darkness, unable to sleep and I thought of Japanese rooms, empty in the center, the spare furnishings against the walls, encircling the middle. How often circles appeared. Geometric mirroring and straight lines were practically nonexistent. Evil spirits, according to Shinto belief, traveled in straight lines.

What had my teacher said? *Hen,* a small circular area, either temporal or conceptual, with no formal boundary. *Atari,* the same, only larger. The circle, the symbol for group, its thin line defining inside and outside. Circles.

In my mind I was still lost, wandering the unnumbered, unnamed streets, following their curves, walking in circles. Their irregularity seemed deliberate, was deliberate. Their routes, I realized, followed the ancient streets that encircled the Emperor's Palace at the heart of the city. They had been laid down in such a way as to befuddle, their curves intended to disorient all those unfamiliar with the place: strangers, invaders, me. I pictured the streets and districts of the ancient Japanese cities growing outward in rings from around the castles at their cores, the intentionally elliptical streets, the modern transit systems that followed them centuries later, circumscribing the core regions.

There was a full moon outside my dormitory window. Its light cast onto the wall and my poster of the Japanese flag. I could see the pristine white field but I could not make out color, only a black abstract there at the center. In my mind's eye, however, I saw the brilliant red, and its perfect roundness.

ACKNOWLEDGMENTS

My gratitude to Fred Bernstein, Jon Cantor, Bobby Rosenberg, Jay Shaw, Carol Spielberger, and Olga Weiser. I wish to express particular appreciation to Elizabeth Hartung and Amy McGinnis for their thoughful criticism. And I thank Josh Schor for his unwavering friendship and support and Vivian Walker for her inspiration and encouragement.

BIBLIOGRAPHY

Barthes, Roland. *Empire of Signs*. New York: Hill and Wang, 1982.

Befu, Harumi. *Japan: An Anthropological Introduction*. Tokyo: Charles E. Tuttle Company Inc., 1971.

Benedict, Ruth. *The Crysanthemum and the Sword*. Tokyo: Charles E. Tuttle Company Inc., 1946.

Bruce-Briggs, B. "The Dangerous Folly Called Theory Z," *Fortune* May 17, 1983, pp. 41–53.

Campbell, Jeremy. *Grammatical Man*. New York: Simon and Schuster, 1982.

Christopher, Robert. *The Japanese Mind*. London: Pan Books Ltd., 1983.

Dalby, Liza. *Geisha*. New York: Vintage Books, 1983.

Discover Japan, Vol 1, 2: Words, Customs and Concepts. Tokyo: Kodansha, 1982.

Doi, Takeo. *The Anatomy of Dependence*. Tokyo: Kodansha, 1973.

Haberman, Clyde. "In Japan Mickey-San Is Right At Home," *The New York Times*, September 25, 1986, p. 37.

Hall, Edward T. *The Silent Language*. Garden City: Anchor Books, 1973.

Hall, Edward T. *The Hidden Dimension*. Garden City: Anchor Books, 1969.

Hall, Edward T. *Beyond Culture*. Garden City: Anchor Books, 1981.

Hall, Edward T. *The Dance of Life*. Garden City: Anchor Books, 1983.

Halloran, Fumiko Mori. "Japan's Shining Prince Turns 1000," *The New York Times Book Review,* November 30, 1986, p. 1.

Hildebrand, John. "How Johnny and Taro Measure Up," *Newsday,* July 8, 1986, Part II, p. 3.

Honna, Nobuyuki and Hoffer, Bates. *An English Dictionary of Japanese Culture.* Tokyo: Yukihaku Publishing Co., 1986.

Imai, Masaaki. *Sixteen Ways to Avoid Saying No.* Tokyo: NIhon Keizai Shimbun, Inc. 1981.

Intensive Course in Japanese. Tokyo: Language Services Company, Ltd., 1983.

"Younger Workers Less Enthusiastic About Work," *The Japan Economic Journal,* August 9, 1986, p. 24.

Kawabata, Yasunari. *Thousand Cranes.* New York: Putnam, 1981.

Kawabata, Yasunari. *Snow Country.* New York: Putnam, 1981.

Kamata, Satoshi. *Japan in the Passing Lane.* New York: Pantheon Books, 1973.

Lakoff, George and Johnson, Mark. *Metaphors We Live By.* Chicago: University of Chicago Press, 1980.

Lynch, Kevin. *The Image of the City.* Cambridge, MA: The M.I.T. Press, 1960.

Lyons, Nick. *The Sony Vision.* New York: Crown Books, 1976.

McQueen, Ian. *Japan: A Travel Survival Kit.* Victoria, Australia: Lonely Planet Publications, 1981.

Main, Jeremy. "The Trouble With Managing Japanese Society," *Fortune,* April 2, 1984, pp. 50–56.

Musashi, Miyamoto. *A Book of Five Rings.* Woodstock, N.Y.: The Overlook Press, 1974.

Nekane, Chie. *Japanese Society.* New York: Penguin Books, 1970.

Natsume, Soseki. *Botchan.* Tokyo: Kodansha, 1980.

Natsume, Soseki. *I Am A Cat, Vol I.* Tokyo and Rutland: Charles E. Tuttle Company, 1972.

Nihongo Notes, Vol 1–5. Tokyo: The Japan Times, Ltd., 1983.

Oe, Kenzaburo. *A Personal Matter.* Tokyo: Charles E. Tuttle Company, 1968.

O'Neill, Gerard. *The Technology Edge.* New York: Simon and Schuster, 1983.

Ouchi, William G. *Theory Z.* Menlo Park, CA: Addison-Wesley Publishing Company, 1981.

Pascale, Richard T. and Athos, Anthony G. *The Art of Japanese Management.* New York: Simon and Schuster, 1981.

Peters, Thomas J. and Waterman Jr., Robert H. *In Search of Excellence.* New York: Warner Books, 1982.

Pinault, Lewis J. "The Suffocating Embrace of Japanese Management," *Technology Review,* October 1984, p. 10–11.

Reischauer, Edwin O. *The Japanese.* Cambridge, MA: The Harvard University Press, 1977.

Restak, Richard. *The Brain.* New York: Bantam Books, Inc., 1984.

"Salarymen" in Japan. Japan: Japan Travel Bureau, Inc., 1987.

Smith, Lee. "Japan's Autocratic Managers," *Fortune,* January 7, 1985, pp. 56–64.

Taylor, Jared. *Shadows of the Rising Sun.* New York: William Morrow, 1983.

Vogel, Ezra. *Japan As Number One: Lessons for America.* Cambridge, MA: Harvard University Press, 1979.

"What Can The Japanese Teach U.S. Management: What Is Transferable to the West and What Is Not." *World Business Weekly,* January 19, 1981.

Whiting, Robert. *The Crysanthemum and the Bat: Baseball Sammurai Style.* New York: Avon, 1983.

Whorf, Benjamin Lee. *Language, Thought, and Reality.* New York: The Technology Press of M.I.T. and John Wiley and Sons, 1956.

Woronoff, Jon. *Japan's Wasted Workers.* Tokyo: Lotus Press Ltd. 1982.

Zimmerman, Mark. *How To Do Business With the Japanese.* New York: Random House, 1985.

Gary J. Katzenstein graduated magna cum laude from Brown University. He holds a Master of Science in Computer Science and a Master of Business Administration, with honors, from the University of California at Los Angeles.

Mr. Katzenstein was a recipient of a Luce Scholarship for work and study in Asia. His most recent visit to the Far East took him to Korea, Taiwan, and Japan. Mr. Katzenstein works as a computer systems consultant and technical writer.